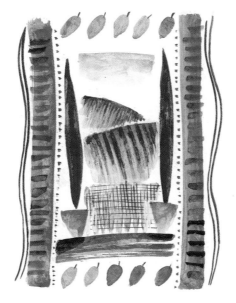

For My Grandmother

Italian Country Cooking

RECIPES FROM UMBRIA & APULIA

SUSANNA GELMETTI

DESIGNED & ILLUSTRATED BY ROBERT BUDWIG
PHOTOGRAPHY BY MIHAI DRAGUTESCU

TEN SPEED PRESS
BERKELEY, CALIFORNIA

Acknowledgements

There are many people who have helped me while I was writing this book. Special thanks go to Mihai Dragutescu for his lovely colour pictures and for the time spent on them both in Italy and in London. My thanks also to the two chefs of my cookery school, Antonio Bondi in Umbria and our magical Tonino Punzi in Apulia, and to everyone at Lo Spagnulo. Thanks to Rosalyn Palmer, Debra Burtt, Carole Seawert, Alan Bannister, Tan Harrington and her team at Richard Mulcaster Associates and Julie Wilkinson at Abercrombie & Kent.

The warmest thanks are for my editor Maureen Green and everyone at Rosendale Press including Barbara Duke, Nasim Mawji and Miranda Green, for having given me such a delightful opportunity and for their efforts in shaping my text, faxing back and forth while I was in Italy teaching at my school. Thanks to Robert Budwig for designing the book and for his delightful drawings. And finally to a very close friend of mine for all the time spent in correcting my mistakes in English and for helping me to find some beautiful sentences.

I would like to take this opportunity to thank all the guests who have come to the cookery school and the many journalists who have visited us there and responded with such enthusiasm. I owe them even more than they know. A last thought goes to the friends for whom I have been cooking since I was young; an endless number of weekends spent in the kitchen while I was unconsciously practising for my future career. My extended family both in Italy and in Nairobi have always been very enthusiastic about good food, and happily supported my passion for cooking. Thanks to "Ceramic Blue", London and "Verandah", London for the loan of many of the plates used in photography.

Copyright © 1996 by Susanna Gelmetti

Photography © 1996 by Mihai Dragutescu
Illustrations © 1996 by Robert Budwig

First published in Great Britain in 1996 by
Rosendale Press Ltd, Premier House
10 Greycoat Place, London SW1P 1SB

Ten Speed Press
Post Office Box 7123
Berkeley, California 94707

Design © 1996 Rosendale Press Limited
Typesetting by Ace Filmsetting Ltd, Frome, Somerset
Origination by Canale & Co. SPA, Turin

Library of Congress Cataloging-in-Publication Data
Gelmetti, Susanna.
Italian country cooking: recipes from Umbria and Puglia / by Susanna Gelmetti; illustrated by Robert Budwig.
p. cm.
Includes index
ISBN 0-89815-828-1

1. Cookery, Italian. 2. Cookery--Italy--Umbria. 3. Cookery--Italy--Puglia. I. Title.
TX723.G354 1996
641.5945--dc20
96-4036
CIP

First Ten Speed Press printing, 1996
Printed in Italy by G. Canale & Co. SPA, Turin

1 2 3 4 5   00 99 98 97 96

Contents

Introduction

Italian food is about the simple combination of very fresh ingredients; cooking, apart from a few notable exceptions, is kept to the minimum, and techniques are straightforward. It is not necessary to contrive complicated flavours in a country brimful of fruit and vegetables, boasting a wide variety of fish, many cheeses, good wines and olive oil that is the envy of the world. Good ingredients have always been available in Italy and Italians never had to go far to find staples. From this they developed an innate confidence in mixing ingredients, experimenting and eventually coming up with inventions such as pasta or pizza.

The separate states of Italy have only come together as a nation in a little over a hundred years, but the great differences between one region and another are not only historical. Different landscapes, climates and neighbouring borders have resulted in very different styles of cooking. Some ingredients available in Apulia will never be found in Rome or Milan. This rich diversity is the beauty of Italian food, and when travelling in Italy there is a thrilling feeling that you are constantly discovering a different country.

The ingredients of Italian cooking developed along with the country's history. The Greeks colonised Apulia and found it so beautiful, fertile and exceptionally easy to cultivate that they called it Magna Graecia. The ancient Romans, Arabs, Spanish and Normans all left signs of their presence, planting different seeds to add to the regional crops. The city state of Venice imported expensive and exotic spices. But however much Italian cooking might vary from one region to another, there are common rules, unwritten traditions, that apply to every family, to every town, to north and south, rich and poor. The form of an Italian meal has existed for centuries, and its focus extends over all courses, rather than falling on one particular high point.

I have chosen to concentrate on the cooking of two regions, Umbria and Apulia (as I do in my cookery school) because of their interesting traditions and the contrast between them. Umbria, the relatively little known neighbour of Tuscany, is a land of beautiful rolling hills, forests, sheep, pigs and truffles. Together with Tuscany it has probably the richest concentration of churches, frescoes and paintings. Its classical landscape pro-

duces delightful wines, delicate olive oils and hearty dishes flavoured with garlic. Apulia, a region right down in the heel of Italy that is now becoming very fashionable, has a style of cooking that is the quintessence of the Mediterranean diet: fresh vegetables, fish, tomatoes, pasta and olive oil everywhere.

These two regions have one thing in common: their cooking developed out of necessity. Days spent working in the fields and orchards left little time for preparing elaborate dishes and yet the importance of food, both as nourishment and as a communal ritual, meant it had to be fresh, delicious and reasonably quick to prepare. A typical mid-week meal in Apulia in winter, for example, might be orecchiette pasta with broccoli, followed by lamb baked with tomatoes, potatoes, rosemary and olive oil – a delightful meal, ready in an hour and followed by a simple dessert, cheese or fruit. At the weekend, the meal might start off with an antipasto; the pasta will often be home-made, filled with ricotta, nutmeg and Parmigiano; roast seabass might then be served with mashed potatoes and herbs; fresh salad with a whole variety of leaves to follow and finally a torta with fresh pears and almonds.

The recipes in this book are mainly Umbrian and Apulian, discovered and enjoyed over many years while running my cookery school, visiting local restaurants, talking to local chefs and local people. Some come from my family; the totally different kind of food that I ate at home with my parents. From them I learnt the pleasure of entertaining friends, of cooking for an endless stream of visitors to the house and a natural taste for good food however simple that might be.

Cooking Italian food is meant to be a happy experience, however much of a novice you may be. The following recipes will suit any and every occasion, are easy to follow and not dependent on rare ingredients. You will gradually acquire confidence in a few basic techniques, and then cook in a relaxed and joyful mood – an essential acompaniment to all Italian food .

Susanna Gelmetti

Antipasti are light introductions to an extended meal, intended to tempt the taste buds and excite the appetite for the courses to follow. They can range from the simple and refreshing, such as ripe figs and prosciutto, to more refined combinations of ricotta and tomato. Antipasti are not intended to be filling, although many of these dishes can be expanded and developed as main courses. In Umbria and in Tuscany the classic antipasto comprises local ham or salami, crostini with chicken livers or bruschetta simply rubbed with garlic and olive oil. In Apulia country people usually prepare an enormously large range of antipasti, from cold frittata to fried black olives with chillies. The common requirement for any kind of antipasto is to use only a few ingredients at a time – always very fresh and the very best quality possible.

Bruschetta con Peperoni Arrosto e Formaggio di Capra

Bruschetta with Red Peppers and Goat's Cheese

The flesh of roast sweet peppers provides a delicious sweetness that melts in the mouth, while the tangy flavour of goat's cheese makes an ideal complement.

2 red sweet peppers (capsicums)
1 yellow sweet pepper (capsicum)
60ml/4 tbsp extra virgin olive oil
Salt and freshly ground black pepper
A generous amount of fresh basil leaves,
*   roughly torn*
4-6 thick slices of country bread, toasted
2 garlic cloves, peeled
Extra virgin olive oil for drizzling
100g/3½oz goat's cheese, roughly chopped

Preheat the oven to 190°C/375°F/gas mark 5.

Put the peppers on an unoiled baking pan and roast them in the oven for 20–30 minutes, until they start to collapse and the skins blacken. Transfer to a bowl and cover with foil to trap moisture. Leave for about 10 minutes until the skin loosens. Peel the peppers, cut open and remove the stem and seeds. Tear the pepper flesh into strips. Dress with olive oil, salt and black pepper, and basil.

Rub the hot bread with the garlic cloves and sprinkle with salt, black pepper and olive oil. Lay the peppers on top and crumble the goat's cheese over them. Dribble over a little more olive oil and serve. Serves 4–6

Bruschetta con Fegatini, Salvia e Ginepro
Chicken Liver Bruschetta with Sage and Juniper Berries

Traditionally this dish would have formed the start of a family meal, with the chicken itself being the main course. However, it is now possible to buy the livers separately from the chicken, in larger quantities. This rough country pâté keeps for up to three days in the refrigerator and makes an instant snack as well as the start to a meal.

45ml/3 tbsp extra virgin olive oil
250g/9oz chicken livers, washed and trimmed
1 tbsp capers, roughly chopped
1 carrot, finely chopped
Juice of ½ lemon, plus the lemon skin
6 fresh sage leaves, coarsely chopped
10 juniper berries, crushed
45ml/3 tbsp dry Marsala or medium dry sherry
180ml/6fl oz (¾ cup) dry white wine
Salt and freshly ground black pepper
4-6 thick slices of country bread, toasted
Extra virgin olive oil for drizzling

Heat the olive oil in a frying pan and add the chicken livers, capers, carrot, lemon skin and juice, sage leaves and juniper berries. Sauté for 5 minutes without browning. Add the Marsala, white wine, salt and black pepper, reduce the heat and simmer for 10–15 minutes, or until cooked.

Remove the lemon skin, and mash the mixture with the back of a fork. Spread on toasted bread, drizzle with olive oil and serve. Serves 4–6

Bruschetta con Zucchine

Bruschetta with Courgettes

The tenderness of the sautéed vegetables combines well with the crunchiness of the toasted bread.

60ml/4 tbsp extra virgin olive oil
1 small onion, finely chopped
3 courgettes (zucchini), cut into 5mm/¼inch
   discs
3 garlic cloves, peeled
2 tbsp finely chopped fresh flat-leaf
   (continental) parsley
Salt and freshly ground black pepper
4-6 thick slices of country bread, toasted
Extra virgin olive oil for drizzling
8 fresh basil leaves, roughly torn

Gently heat the olive oil in a small frying pan. Add the onion and sauté for 10 minutes, until soft and translucent. Crush 2 of the garlic cloves and add with the courgettes and parsley to the onion. Cover the pan and cook over a medium heat for 15–20 minutes, stirring frequently, until the courgettes become soft. If they char slightly, so much the better. Season with salt and black pepper.

Rub each of the hot bread slices with the remaining peeled garlic clove and drizzle with olive oil. Mix the basil with the courgettes and serve on top of the bread. Serves 4–6

Zucchine Incartocciate

Grilled Courgette and Goat's Cheese Parcels

Grilled courgettes, like grilled aubergines, have become very fashionable of late. I still like them for all that. Here they are served with goat's cheese, lemon juice and olive oil, and are even better. Again, this dish can be prepared in advance.

6 medium courgettes (zucchini), sliced thinly
lengthways
300g/10½oz hard goat's cheese, diced
Grated zest and juice of 1 lemon
A small bunch of fresh flat-leaf (continental)
parsley, chopped
A small bunch of fresh basil leaves, roughly
torn
45-60ml/3-4 tbsp extra virgin olive oil
Salt and freshly ground black pepper

Preheat a ridged grill pan on top of the stove for about 10 minutes. Grill the courgette slices until tender and lightly browned on both sides.

In a bowl, mix the cubes of cheese with the lemon zest and some of the chopped herbs, tossing to coat the cheese. Place a piece of cheese on each courgette slice. Roll up and secure with a toothpick. Put the rolls into a bowl and drizzle over a little olive oil and the lemon juice. Sprinkle with the remaining herbs and season with salt and black pepper. Refrigerate for 30 minutes. If preparing in advance, leave in the refrigerator covered with plastic film.

When ready to serve, add a little extra fresh lemon juice and black pepper and stir gently. Serves 4–6

Crostini con Fagioli Borlotti, Cipolla Rossa e Olive Nere

Crostini with Borlotti Beans, Red Onion and Black Olives

Crostini are more elegant and less substantial than bruschetta, a nibble rather than a hearty snack, perfect served as an accompaniment to drinks. French baguette or Italian bastone are cut diagonally into thin slices, making a light base for a more delicate topping. The bread can be toasted in advance and will remain crisp for several days, but only add the topping just before serving. Borlotti beans are one of the creamiest of the pulses. Resist the temptation to use the canned variety. The pleasure of this dish is in the flavour of the beans.

300g/10½oz (1½ cups) dried borlotti beans, soaked overnight
1 red onion, chopped
Salt
1 French baguette or Italian bastone
90ml/6 tbsp extra virgin olive oil
Freshly ground black pepper
A few drops of red wine or balsamic vinegar
50g/2oz (⅓ cup) black olives
1 tbsp chopped fresh flat-leaf (continental) parsley

Preheat the oven to 200°C/400°F/gas mark 6.

Drain the beans, cover with plenty of fresh water and simmer until tender; check them after 30 minutes although they could take up to an hour. Don't add salt to the water as this will make the beans tough. When cooked, drain the beans and mash half of them with the back of a fork.

If you are concerned about the strength of the raw onion, put the chopped onion in a sieve, sprinkle over a generous quantity of salt and leave for 2 minutes; rinse under cold water and proceed with the recipe.

Cut the bread into 1cm/½ inch slices. If this is done diagonally, rather than straight across the loaf, it looks more attractive.

Arrange the slices on a wire rack in a roasting pan. Dribble a little olive oil over the slices; don't worry if the oil doesn't appear to cover all the bread – the heat of the oven will do that for you. Toast, turning once, at the top of the pre-heated oven for about 10 minutes or until golden. Watch carefully, as golden turns to dark brown very quickly.

Mix the onion with both the mashed and the whole beans. Add half the olive oil, season with salt and black pepper, and add a few drops of vinegar. Place the beans on top of the crostini, dribble over the remaining olive oil, top with a few black olives and sprinkle with parsley. Serves 4–6

Olive Nere Soffritte e Mozzarella

Fried Black Olives and Mozzarella

*Hot olives are surprisingly different from cold, the texture fleshier and the
flavour sweeter. Serve them as in this recipe with best-quality buffalo
mozzarella, or sprinkled over a salad.*

200g/7oz ripe tomatoes
45-60ml/3-4 tbsp extra virgin olive oil
1 garlic clove, chopped
300g/10½oz (2 cups) black olives, pitted
1½ tsp chopped fresh oregano
2 fresh hot red chillies, finely chopped
Salt and freshly ground black pepper
300g/10½oz buffalo mozzarella cheese

Make a cross with a sharp knife at the base
of each tomato, just to split the skin. Plunge
the tomatoes into boiling water for 1 minute,
or until the cross at the base starts to open up.
Remove with a slotted spoon and peel off the
skin, which should come away easily with a
sharp knife. Remove core and seeds and
roughly chop the flesh.

Heat the olive oil in a frying pan and sauté
the garlic for 1 minute, then add the tomatoes
and simmer for 2 minutes. Add the olives,
oregano and chillies and season with salt and
black pepper. Heat through and serve hot,
with a few thick slices of mozzarella on the
side and some good country bread. Serves 4

Sformatini di Ricotta e Pomodoro

Ricotta Moulds and Basil with Fresh Tomato Sauce

Really ripe red tomatoes and the freshest ricotta you can find are the essence of this dish. The scent and flavour of basil is one of the greatest pleasures of summer.

8 ripe plum tomatoes
Salt and freshly ground black pepper
90ml/6 tbsp extra virgin olive oil
A generous amount of fresh basil leaves,
*   roughly torn*
300g/10½oz (1¼ cups) fresh ricotta cheese
A few fresh basil leaves to garnish

Make a cross with a sharp knife at the base of each tomato, just to split the skin. Plunge the tomatoes into boiling water for 1 minute, or until the cross at the base starts to open up. Remove with a slotted spoon and peel off the skin, which should come away easily with a sharp knife. Remove core and seeds. Work the tomato flesh in a food processor for 15–20 seconds, until smooth but not completely mashed. Season with salt and black pepper.

Add half of the olive oil and 5 torn basil leaves.

In a bowl mix the ricotta with a generous seasoning of salt and black pepper and the remaining torn basil. Spread the tomato sauce equally over four flat plates. Mould the ricotta into balls, using two spoons dipped in cold water. Arrange two ricotta balls per person on top of the tomato sauce. Add a generous dribbling of olive oil and extra basil leaves to garnish, and serve. Serves 4

Panzanella

Salad of Tomatoes, Garlic and Country Bread

This famous Tuscan salad was traditionally eaten by shepherds and intended to be a meal in itself. Nothing is more delicious than raw, fresh, crunchy vegetables dressed in good extra virgin olive oil. The country bread binds together all the different textures, colours and flavours.

1 red sweet pepper (capsicum)
1 yellow sweet pepper (capsicum)
2 carrots
2 small red onions
2 cucumbers
2 ripe beef tomatoes
2 celery stalks
2 tender fennel bulbs
200g/7oz stale country bread
Salt and freshly ground black pepper
45ml/3 tbsp red wine vinegar
180ml/6fl oz (¾ cup) extra virgin olive oil
1 garlic clove, finely chopped
Fresh basil leaves, roughly torn

Chop all the vegetables into cubes of about 1cm/½ inch and place in a large bowl. Soak the bread in cold water until softened, then squeeze the water out and crumble the bread by hand into the vegetables. Mix together. Season with salt and black pepper, then add the vinegar, olive oil, garlic and basil leaves. Toss the salad thoroughly. This dish needs to rest for 30 minutes in a cool place before serving, to allow the flavours to infuse. Serves 4–6

Fichi e Prosciutto di Parma

Parma Ham with Figs

A plate of thinly cut country ham and olives, or a mixture of thick-cut salami served with or without sweet fruity accompaniments, is one of the most popular ways to start an Italian meal. In this recipe, the thinnest slices of tender Parma ham are combined with ripe figs for a simple taste of summer.

60g/2oz very thinly sliced Parma ham
(prosciutto) per person
1 or 2 fresh figs per person

Arrange the Parma ham across the plate without breaking the delicate mixture of fat and lean. Wash the figs and arrange alongside. Serve with good country bread.

Insalata di Finocchi

Fennel Salad

This is a light salad with a distinctive delicate flavour. It is delicious when prepared a little in advance.

2 small tender fennel bulbs
45ml/3 tbsp extra virgin olive oil
Juice of ½ lemon
Salt and freshly ground black pepper

Trim the top and base of the fennel, and remove any coarse outside leaves. Holding the bulb firmly, cut thin slices vertically. Mix the fennel slices with the olive oil and season with salt and black pepper. Set aside for at least 15 minutes and pour the lemon juice over it before serving. Serves 4

Frittata con Cipolle Rosse

Red Onion Frittata

Fritatta is half-way between an omelette and a soufflé, and eaten all over Italy. The traditional frittata of Apulia is highly original. In the south they add coarse breadcrumbs to the eggs and vegetables, giving the dish more body and an interesting slightly crunchy texture. I suggest you serve it with a light fennel salad (see page 21). Frittata even tastes good cold the next day.

500g/1lb red onions, cut into semi-circle slices
45ml/3 tbsp extra virgin olive oil
8 eggs
50g/2oz (½ cup) freshly grated Parmigiano
*   Reggiano – the best Parmesan cheese*
50g/2oz (½ cup) fresh breadcrumbs
1 tbsp chopped fresh flat-leaf (continental)
*   parsley*
Salt and freshly ground black pepper

Preheat the oven to 190°C/375°F/gas mark 5.

Lightly oil a cake pan 25cm/10 inches in diameter, preferably one with detachable sides.

Heat the olive oil and sauté the onions for 15 minutes, until tender, stirring so that they do not burn. Set aside to cool. Lightly beat the eggs in a bowl and then work in the cheese, breadcrumbs, parsley and, finally, the cooked onions. Season with salt and black pepper.

Pour the mixture into the lightly oiled cake pan and bake for 15 minutes, or until the frittata rises and forms a golden crust.

Remove from the oven and allow to subside for 5 minutes. Remove from the pan while still warm, and cut into slices. Serve with a little fennel salad on the side. Serves 6–8

Making Perfect Pizza

A wedge of hot pizza with a glass of wine frequently appears as an opening bite before Italian dinners or as a last minute late night snack, but never at mid-day. Of course, a whole pizza can provide an informal supper all by itself. Home-made Italian pizza has a light, airy crust, the thinner the better, and is no more difficult to make than any other kind of bread. Pizza must be served very hot, straight from the oven, to be really appetising.

For the pizza crust:
15g/½ oz fresh yeast or 1½ tsp dried yeast
300ml/½ pint (1¼ cups) warm water
500g/1lb plain flour (3⅔ cups all-purpose
   flour), plus more for rolling out
2 tsp salt
1 tsp sugar
15ml/1 tbsp extra virgin olive oil

This recipe should make four small pizzas (about 23cm/9 inches each) or two the size of a standard baking sheet.

Dissolve the yeast in about half a glass of the warm water, or according to the directions on the packet.

Sift three quarters of the flour into a large bowl and hollow out a well in the middle of it. Add the salt, sugar, olive oil and yeast mixture. Using your fingers, work the ingredients in the well together, then incorporate the flour from the edges, gradually adding the remaining water and keeping the mixture in the middle runny and sticky. When all the ingredients have been mixed in you should be left with a mass of sticky dough.

Flour a big board liberally to prevent any sticking, and pour the dough on to it. Add the remaining flour to the dough and work it in. Fold the dough in from the edges and then knead outwards. You may need to add more flour. Keep turning the mass of dough and

working it evenly. Flour any sticky bits; scrape the board of any bits that are sticking and work them in. Keep the surface well floured. Kneading the dough requires quite a lot of effort and should be done for about 20 minutes in order to activate the yeast and the gluten in the flour. Really lean into your kneading, stretching the dough away from you with the heel of your hands and continually turning it so that it is worked evenly, in all directions. After about 5 minutes, the dough should stop absorbing flour and start to become drier, more of a solid mass. The sides will become smooth in texture. You may still need to rub a little flour into the dough to stop any sticking. When the kneading is finished, fold the edges under to make a smooth mound. Rub some flour into the top, then put the dough in a bowl and cover it with a damp cloth. Leave in a warm place to rise for 2 hours. The dough should double in size.

While the dough is rising, prepare the

toppings so they will be ready when the dough has been rolled out. Once the dough has risen, preheat the oven to 240°C/475°F/gas mark 9. If you are using a baking stone, put it in the oven to heat up. Oil two baking sheets with olive oil.

Divide the dough into four small balls or into two larger balls. Roll out each ball of dough on a well-floured surface, using a lightly floured rolling pin. Keep flouring, and picking up and turning the dough over, rolling on both sides. The consistency should be wonderfully stretchy and elastic. Roll out quite thinly, aiming for pizza bases of 5mm/¼ inch thickness, and about the shape of your baking sheets if making two larger pizzas. Transfer the dough to the baking sheets and cut off any excess. You may find that the dough shrinks back a bit into the baking sheet but do try to keep some edges.

The following are six suggested pizza toppings:

Mozzarella and Tomato

225g/8oz mozzarella cheese, diced
10 cherry tomatoes, halved
A handful of fresh basil leaves

Ricotta and Rocket (Arugula)

150g/5oz (about ⅔ cup) ricotta cheese
10 cherry tomatoes, halved
A handful of rocket (arugula), roughly torn

Mozzarella and Porcini

225g/8oz mozzarella cheese, diced
50g/2oz dried porcini mushrooms, soaked in 600ml/1 pint (2½ cups) hot water for about 30 minutes, then chopped
A handful of rocket (arugula), roughly torn

Mozzarella and Pancetta

225g/8oz mozzarella cheese, diced and mixed with 90ml/6 tbsp single (light) cream
100g/3½ oz *pancetta*, thinly sliced
Freshly ground black pepper

Mozzarella and Rocket (Arugula)

110g/4oz mozzarella cheese, diced
75g/2½oz (about ⅓ cup) ricotta cheese
A handful of rocket (arugula), roughly torn

Spread the cheese evenly over the pizza base, then add either the tomatoes, mushrooms or pancetta, and drizzle with olive oil. Bake in the hottest part of the oven for ·10–15 minutes or until the base and edge of the crust are crisp and golden brown. Add the rocket, basil salt and black pepper and serve immediately.

Tomato, Basil and Mozzarella

300g/10½ oz (1¼ cups) chopped tomatoes
15ml/1 tbsp extra virgin olive oil
A few fresh basil leaves, roughly torn
A pinch of salt
225g/8oz mozzarella cheese, diced
A handful of rocket (arugula), roughly torn

Mix the tomatoes, olive oil, basil and salt together in a bowl and spread evenly over the pizza base. Follow this with the mozzarella, and drizzle with more olive oil. Bake in the hottest part of the oven for 10–15 minutes or until the edge and base of the crust are crisp and golden brown. Add the rocket and serve immediately. Serves 4–6

Budino di Parmigiano

Parmesan Mould

*The rich flavour of freshly grated Parmigiano Reggiano cheese is one of the
most exquisite themes of Italian cooking. Here the combination of this
wonderful cheese with cream and black pepper creates a very special dish,
simple to prepare, but with a very sophisticated flavour.*

4 egg yolks
50g/2oz plain flour (2 tbsp all-purpose flour)
200g/7oz (1¼ cups) freshly grated
Parmigiano Reggiano
300ml/½ pint (1¼ cups) milk
300ml/½ pint single cream (1¼ cups light cream)
Salt and freshly ground black pepper

Preheat the oven to 180°C/350°F/gas mark 4.

Whisk the egg yolks for a few minutes. Then add the flour, cheese, milk and cream and continue to whisk. Finally, season well, remembering that the Parmesan is already salty.

Oil a glass or china oven-proof mould of 1.2 litres/2 pints (5 cups) capacity and pour in the cheese mixture. Place the mould in a bain-marie, or roasting pan half-filled with warm water, and bake for 30 minutes, until the mixture thickens. Remove and allow to cool a little.

Serve warm from the mould, accompanied by a simple rocket (arugula) salad or the tomato sauce on page 90. Serves 6–8

Primi piatti.

Suggest Italian food and everyone immediately thinks of pasta. The pasta craze has now conquered the world. Healthy as well as simple to make, pasta now appears on virtually every restaurant menu and is among the staples of any kitchen cupboard. Gradually, everyone has learned that texture is all important, and that pasta must be served al dente, or firm to the bite. In authentic Italian cooking, pasta is one of the basic ingredients for the first course or primi piatti. Pasta, risotto or a nourishing soup will be followed by a main course of meat or fish, with vegetables. Pasta was never meant to be served on its own – an Italian would find this a bit desperate! Stick to a good Italian brand of dried pasta and learn to make the fresh version yourself. Although often approached with trepidation by the non-Italian cook, pasta, gnocchi di patate and risotti are well-loved primi piatti that can be achieved with a little practice.

Acqua Cotta

Fresh Tomato Soup with Onions and Basil

A classic Tuscan soup, this dish is well known and eaten all over Italy in summer. Simplicity itself, the name means 'cooked water'. All that is required is fresh, ripe tomatoes, fresh basil and good olive oil. It is one of the many summer soups which are also very good eaten cold the next day, adding the bread when you actually serve the soup.

500g/1lb ripe tomatoes
90ml/6 tbsp extra virgin olive oil
1kg/2lb onions, chopped
200g/7oz fatty Parma ham (prosciutto) or
  unsmoked bacon, chopped
Salt and freshly ground black pepper
A generous amount of fresh basil leaves,
  roughly torn
1.2 litres/2 pints (5 cups) water
4-6 slices of fresh country bread, cut into
  small pieces
100g/3½oz (1 cup) freshly grated
  Parmigiano Reggiano - the best
  Parmesan cheese
Extra virgin olive oil for drizzling

Make a cross with a sharp knife at the base of each tomato, just to split the skin. Plunge the tomatoes into boiling water for 1 minute, or until the cross at the base starts to open up. Remove with a slotted spoon and peel off the skin, which should come away easily with a sharp knife. Remove core and seeds, and roughly chop the flesh.

Heat the olive oil in a large saucepan and sauté the onions until soft, then add the chopped ham or bacon, salt and black pepper.

Add the chopped tomatoes to this mixture along with the basil and water. Leave to cook for about 1 hour, simmering gently with the lid on. Stir from time to time.

Meanwhile, toast the bread and use to line the bottom of a large serving bowl. Pour the soup into the bowl, sprinkle with the Parmesan, season with more salt and black pepper and drizzle with olive oil. Leave for 5 minutes before serving. Serves 6

Minestra di Pasta e Lenticchie

Lentil and Pasta Soup

Think of lentils, and one immediately thinks of autumn and winter approaching. In Italy lentils are cooked from October until February and especially on New Year's day. These traditional legumes in which Umbria is so rich are supposed to represent money, and prosperity in the year to come. The smaller the lentils the better.

45ml/3 tbsp extra virgin olive oil
2 garlic cloves, chopped
2 small fresh hot red chillies, chopped
2 carrots, diced small
1 celery stalk, diced small
250g/9oz (1¼ cups) green lentils, soaked for
   a few hours and drained
180ml/6fl oz (¾ cup) white wine
1.2 litres/2 pints (5 cups) water
150g/5oz dried egg tagliolini, broken into pieces
Salt and freshly ground black pepper
2 tbsp chopped fresh flat-leaf (continental)
   parsley
50g/2oz (½ cup) freshly grated Parmigiano
   Reggiano – the best Parmesan cheese
Extra virgin olive oil for drizzling

Heat the olive oil in a large pan and sauté the garlic, chillies, carrots and celery for 10 minutes. Then add the lentils. Cook for 5 minutes, stirring from time to time. Add the wine and water and cook with the lid on for a further 20–30 minutes, until the lentils are tender.

Add the pasta and cook for 5 minutes longer. Season well, scatter with chopped parsley and Parmesan, and drizzle with olive oil. The consistency should be that of a thick broth. Serves 4–6

Pasta, Fagioli e Cozze

Bean Soup with Mussels and Pasta

This unusual combination was invented in the area of Naples about ten years ago. The addition of mussels and chillies to the classic Venetian recipe of pasta and beans transforms the dish into something completely different, a delicious southern seafood pasta, with the consistency of a thick soup. It is equally good cold the next day.

350g/12oz (2 cups) dried white beans, such
     as cannellini
6 tbsp chopped fresh flat-leaf (continental)
     parsley
6 ripe tomatoes, chopped
1 onion, chopped
Salt
180ml/6fl oz (¾ cup) extra virgin olive oil
300g/10oz fresh mussels
2 garlic cloves, chopped
2 fresh hot red chillies, deseeded and chopped
200g/7oz dried fettuccine, broken into pieces
Freshly ground black pepper

Soak the beans overnight. The next day, drain them and put in a pan with plenty of fresh water, 2 tbsp of the parsley, 2 tomatoes, the onion, and 60ml/4 tbsp of the olive oil. Cook for 30–40 minutes, until the beans are tender. Mash or process one third of the beans and leave the rest whole.

To clean the mussels, scrub the shells thoroughly, scraping off any barnacles and cutting off the 'beards'. Discard any mussels with broken shells, or any that seem abnormally heavy or float to the top of the cleaning water. Put the cleaned mussels in a saucepan with about 5mm/¼ inch of water, cover and bring to the boil. The shells should have all steamed open in 5–10 minutes; discard any

that still remain closed. Remove the mussels from their shells.

In a big saucepan, heat 60ml/4 tbsp of olive oil and sauté the shelled mussels with the garlic, chillies and 2 tbsp parsley for about 5 minutes. Add the beans, both mashed and whole, with about 600ml/1 pint (2½ cups) of their cooking water, plus the rest of the chopped tomatoes, and stir gently. Finally, add the pieces of pasta and cook for about 4 minutes over a moderate heat, stirring frequently.

Remove from the heat, sprinkle with the remaining chopped parsley and a grinding of black pepper, drizzle with olive oil, and serve. Serves 4–6

Pasta al Pesto

Pasta with Pesto Sauce

This must be one of the best known of all Italian pasta dishes. If your experience of pesto comes from the ready made variety, then head for the nearest market and buy as many bunches of fresh basil as you can lay your hands on! The quintessential Italian combination of olive oil, Parmesan cheese and plenty of aromatic basil is here at its most intense. This sauce keeps well in the refrigerator for a few days, sealed with olive oil and covered with plastic film. Imaginative cooks will find that pesto can be a very versatile partner to many other dishes – as a topping for soups, crostini, or grilled vegetables.

½ tsp coarse sea salt
100g/4oz (about 2½ cups) fresh basil leaves
2 garlic cloves
150ml/¼ pint (⅔ cup) extra virgin olive oil
50g/2oz (⅓ cups) pine nuts
75g/3oz (¾ cup) freshly grated Parmigiano
Freshly ground black pepper
400g/14oz fresh or dried long pasta:
    spaghetti, egg fettuccine or tagliatelle; see
    page 52 for making perfect fresh pasta
Salt
50g/2oz (½ cup) freshly grated Parmigiano
Extra virgin olive oil

Smaller amounts of pesto can be made with a pestle and mortar, which is the traditional procedure and not too time-consuming, but you can also produce a very good pesto in the food processor.

Whichever method you use, first mix the coarse sea salt with the basil and garlic; the salt keeps the basil green and vibrant in colour. Keep mixing, adding the olive oil a little at a time, and then slowly add the pine nuts, Parmesan and black pepper. In a food processor you shouldn't need to mix it for longer than about 2 minutes – and the quicker you can do it the better. The sauce should be a pulpy consistency but still quite rough in texture. Cover with olive oil and leave for 30 minutes in the refrigerator before using.

Cook the pasta in plenty of lightly salted boiling water until *al dente*. Drain the pasta, saving a little of the cooking water to add to the pesto sauce. In a large bowl, toss the pasta with the pesto and a little of the cooking water, along with more Parmesan and olive oil. Make sure that each strand is well coated. Sprinkle with black pepper and serve immediately. Serves 4–6

Gnocchetti con Salsiccia

Gnocchetti with Sausage

This is a wonderful marriage of textures and flavours. The sausage is refined by the subtle hint of saffron and the smooth texture of the aubergine and cream. Rich and delicate, yet hearty at the same time.

60ml/4 tbsp extra virgin olive oil
1 garlic clove, chopped
1 aubergine (eggplant), peeled and diced
200g/7oz Italian luganega *sausage, or the*
*   best Cumberland or pure pork sausage,*
*   skin removed*
300ml/½ pint single cream (1¼ cups light cream)
Salt and freshly ground black pepper
¼ tsp saffron, powdered or strands soaked in
*   a little warm milk*
1 tbsp each chopped fresh flat-leaf (continental)
*   parsley, sage and marjoram*
400g/14oz dried gnocchetti, conchiglie or penne
50g/2oz (½ cup) freshly grated Parmigiano
*   Reggiano - the best Parmesan cheese*

In a large frying pan heat the olive oil with the garlic and then sauté the diced aubergine until tender but still firm. Crumble the sausage into this and cook for 5–10 minutes. Reduce the heat under the sauce and add the cream, salt, black pepper, saffron and all the herbs. Cook for about 3 minutes, stirring well to make sure that the sauce does not stick to the pan. Set aside.

Cook the pasta in plenty of lightly salted boiling water until *al dente*. Drain and add to the sauce. Toss all together adding a little of the pasta cooking water if necessary and serve immediately with a sprinkling of fresh Parmesan. Serves 4–6

Pennette all Boscaiola
Penne with Mushrooms and Sausage

*This is a hearty autumn dish which I first ate in Orvieto in the kitchen of
Antonia, an inspiringly plump Umbrian cook who has helped us for many
summers during our Cookery Weeks. Antonia is an intuitive cook with an
innate confidence in how to handle many ingredients and create dishes which
are different every time she makes them.*

*75g/3oz (6 tbsp) butter
1 onion, finely chopped
1 garlic clove, finely chopped
50g/2oz dried porcini mushrooms, soaked in
    hot water for 1 hour
2 Italian* luganega *sausages, about 200g/7oz, or
    the best Cumberland or pure pork sausage
180ml/6fl oz (¾ cup) white wine
Salt and freshly ground black pepper
400g/14oz penne, or any short dried pasta
Freshly grated Parmigiano Reggiano - the
    best Parmesan cheese*

In a frying pan, heat the butter and sauté
the onion and garlic until soft. Drain the
mushrooms of their soaking water, saving the
water. Squeeze dry and chop. Skin and crumble the sausages and add to the pan along with
the mushrooms, the white wine and 45ml/3
tbsp of the mushroom water, carefully strained.
Cook for about 15 minutes, stirring from time
to time. Add salt and black pepper, if necessary.

Cook the pasta in plenty of lightly salted
boiling water until *al dente*. Drain and toss in
a warm bowl with the sauce. Sprinkle generously with fresh Parmesan and more black
pepper. Serve immediately. Serves 4–6

Conchiglie con Ricotta e Pomodorini

Pasta Shells with Ricotta and Tomatoes

This pasta brings back memories of glorious summer evenings. Long dinners spent chatting until the candles have gone out and then realising that it's nearly morning anyway, so what could be better than a warm, delicious-smelling plate of pasta which can be ready in 15 minutes and so easy that anyone still up can make it?

4 ripe tomatoes, chopped
90ml/6 tbsp extra virgin olive oil
A generous amount of fresh basil leaves,
*   roughly torn*
Salt and freshly ground black pepper
100g/3½ oz (scant ½ cup) fresh ricotta cheese
400g/14oz pasta shells, or other similarly
*   shaped dried pasta*
100g/3½oz (1 cup) freshly grated Parmigiano
*   Reggiano*
Extra virgin olive oil for drizzling

In a large bowl mix the tomatoes, olive oil, basil, salt and black pepper together. Leave to infuse for at least 15 minutes, then add the ricotta. Cook the pasta in plenty of lightly salted boiling water until *al dente*. Drain and toss together with the tomato and ricotta. Sprinkle generously with Parmesan and drizzle with olive oil. Serves 4–6

Gnocchetti alla Paesana

Gnocchetti Umbrian Style

This rich Umbrian dish is traditionally served as part of Sunday lunch.
Prepare, as many Italians do, more sauce than you actually need for the dish
and keep the rest covered in the refrigerator as sauce for a last minute pasta
during the week.

60ml/4 tbsp extra virgin olive oil
100g/3½oz smoked bacon, diced
150g/5oz boneless veal, minced (ground) or
  finely chopped
1 carrot, chopped
1 onion, chopped
1 celery stalk, chopped
180ml/6fl oz (¾cup) white wine
400g/14oz (1¼ cups) fresh tomatoes, chopped
Salt
400g/14oz gnocchetti, or any short dried pasta
100g/3½ oz (1 cup) freshly grated Parmigiano
  Reggiano - the best Parmesan cheese
Freshly ground black pepper

In a casserole, heat the olive oil and sauté the bacon, veal, carrot, onion and celery for about 15 minutes. Add the wine and stir until it almost completely evaporates. Add the tomatoes and cook for a further 10 or 15 minutes. Season with salt.

Cook the gnocchetti in plenty of lightly salted boiling water until *al dente*. Drain and toss with the sauce, mixing well. Sprinkle with Parmesan and black pepper and serve. Serves 4–6

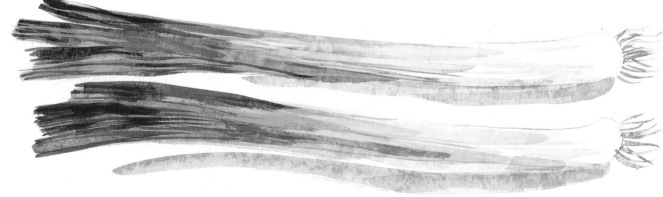

Fettuccine con Uova e Verdure

Fettuccine with Eggs and Vegetables

The more famous version of this Roman dish is pasta alla carbonara, *with a sauce of eggs, bacon and Parmesan. This one follows the same idea but uses vegetables instead of bacon, which imparts a fresher and lighter taste.*

200g/7oz broccoli, trimmed into little florets
60ml/4 tbsp extra virgin olive oil
2 courgettes (zucchini), diced
1 leek, diced
1 carrot, diced
1 red sweet pepper (capsicum), diced
A generous amount of fresh basil leaves,
*   roughly torn*
Salt
3 eggs
50g/2oz (½ cup) freshly grated Parmigiano
*   Reggiano*
350g/12oz dried egg fettuccine
Freshly ground black pepper

Cook the broccoli florets in salted boiling water for about 3–5 minutes, until they are just tender but still firm, then drain and reserve. Heat the olive oil in a large frying pan and sauté all the other vegetables for about 8 minutes. Add the broccoli and, finally, the basil and season with salt. Keep warm.

In a large bowl beat the eggs and the Parmesan together. Cook the pasta in plenty of lightly salted boiling water until *al dente*. Drain the pasta and add to the vegetables. Stir well and quickly add the egg and Parmesan mixture. Toss all together, sprinkle with black pepper and serve immediately. Serves 4

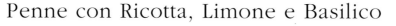

Penne con Ricotta, Limone e Basilico

Penne with Ricotta, Lemon and Basil

A very refreshing pasta, wonderful followed by a salad of mixed leaves with plenty of fennel, carrots, spring onions (scallions) and maybe the red onion frittata on page 23. This is a light summer dinner to impress all your vegetarian friends, and it can be prepared in under half an hour. Remember to buy the freshest ricotta available. You can finish with the gloriously decadent stuffed peaches on page 118.

200g/7oz (scant 1 cup) fresh ricotta cheese
Thinly pared zest of 1 lemon, finely chopped
Salt and freshly ground black pepper
A generous amount of fresh basil leaves,
  roughly torn
400g/14oz penne or any short dried pasta
50g/2oz (½ cup) freshly grated Parmigiano
  Reggiano
Extra virgin olive oil for drizzling

In a large bowl beat the ricotta with the lemon zest using a balloon whisk, adding salt, black pepper and the basil. Cook the pasta in plenty of lightly salted boiling water. Add a ladle of water from the pasta to the ricotta mixture to moisten it a little and then place the bowl over the pasta pan for a few minutes to soften the mixture. When the pasta is *al dente* drain it and mix with the ricotta. Sprinkle with the Parmesan and drizzle with a little olive oil. Serves 4

Cavatelli con Spinaci e Ricotta

Pasta with Spinach and Fresh Ricotta

This Apulian pasta dish is very easy to make anywhere. As with so many pasta dishes, the simplicity of the ingredients and ease of preparation assure a delightful result. The tomato sauce here can be used for many pasta dishes. Sealed with some olive oil and covered with plastic film, it keeps very well in the refrigerator for a couple of days.

300g/10oz (1⅔ cups) spinach
Salt
300g/10oz (1¼ cups) fresh ricotta cheese
*400g/14oz Apulian cavatelli or any short
   dried pasta*
60ml/4 tbsp single (light) cream
*75g/3oz (¾ cup) freshly grated Parmigiano
   Reggiano – the best Parmesan cheese*
Freshly ground black pepper
For the tomato sauce:
*6 fresh ripe tomatoes or 1 x 400g/14oz can
   chopped (crushed) tomatoes*
60ml/4 tbsp extra virgin olive oil
½ onion, finely chopped
Fresh basil leaves, roughly torn
Salt and freshly ground black pepper

First make the tomato sauce. To peel fresh tomatoes, make a cross with a sharp knife at the base of each tomato, just to split the skin. Plunge the tomatoes into boiling water for 1 minute, or until the cross at the base starts to open up. Remove with a slotted spoon and peel off the skin, which should come away easily with a sharp knife. Remove core and seeds, and chop the flesh.

Heat the olive oil and sauté the onion for about 4 minutes. When it becomes translucent, add the chopped tomatoes and cook for a further 10 minutes, or 20 minutes for canned tomatoes. Remove from the heat. Add the basil and season with salt and black pepper.

Wash the spinach and cook in a covered pan with 30ml/2 tbsp water and ½ tsp salt over a gentle heat for about 2 minutes. Watch carefully because spinach can catch easily. Drain thoroughly and chop. Add the spinach and the ricotta to the tomato sauce.

Cook the pasta in plenty of lightly salted boiling water until *al dente*. Drain and toss in the pan with the spinach mixture. Add the cream, Parmesan and black pepper and serve immediately. Serves 4–6

Fettuccine ai Fiori di Zucchine

Fettuccine with Courgette Flowers

Apart from being one of the prettiest of pasta dishes this is also extremely good to eat and simple to make. In Italy in the summer you can buy large bunches of courgette flowers, but they are harder to find elsewhere unless you grow your own. The yellow of these delicate flowers gives the pasta a fantastic golden colour, evocative of Mediterranean warmth and sunlight.

18 courgette (zucchini) flowers, wiped
50g/2oz (4 tbsp) butter
½ onion, chopped
125g/4oz Parma ham (prosciutto) or
    unsmoked bacon, diced
Salt and freshly ground black pepper
350g/12oz dried egg fettuccine
125g/4oz (1 cup) freshly grated Parmigiano
    Reggiano

Using a sharp knife, make a fine slit down one side of each courgette flower so that it can be opened out. Pull the stalk and whole stamen out and discard. Wipe the flowers carefully and cut into strips.

In a large frying pan, heat the butter and sauté the onion and ham for about 10 minutes, until both are translucent. Add the chopped flowers and cook for a further 2 minutes, then season and reduce the heat so the mixture is just kept warm.

Cook the fettuccine in plenty of lightly salted boiling water until *al dente*. Drain and toss in the frying pan with the sauce. Sprinkle with the Parmesan and serve immediately.
Serves 4

Orecchiette con Broccoli

Apulian Pasta with Broccoli

An Apulian pasta par excellence. *The practice of boiling the pasta with vegetables is something which can also be done with spinach, peas and trimmed courgettes (zucchini). Because of the broccoli and the anchovies, this dish is very filling and only needs a good green salad and a cheese board to follow.*

400g/14oz Apulian orecchiette or any short dried pasta
500g/1lb broccoli, trimmed into small florets
90ml/6 tbsp extra virgin olive oil
1 garlic clove, chopped
50g/2oz canned anchovies in olive oil, drained
2 fresh hot red chillies, chopped
Freshly grated Parmigiano Reggiano - the best Parmesan cheese
or 4 tbsp breadcrumbs fried in about
15ml/1 tbsp olive oil until golden

Cook the pasta and broccoli florets in plenty of lightly salted boiling water until the pasta is al dente. Meanwhile, in a large saucepan, heat the olive oil and sauté the garlic with the anchovies and the chilli peppers. Add the drained pasta and broccoli, mix together and sauté for a further 5 minutes. Sprinkle with Parmesan or breadcrumbs and serve. Serves 4–6

Trenette con Gamberi e Fave

Trenette with Prawns and Broad Beans

A spring dish for when fresh broad beans come into season. This very lovely recipe seems to recreate the flavours of the new season with a subtle hint of shellfish. The beans with their skins removed are a delightful colour.

250g/9oz broad (fava) beans, shelled
1 large garlic clove, peeled
75ml/5 tbsp extra virgin olive oil
Salt
1 small onion, chopped
150g/5oz uncooked prawns, shrimp or
*   scampi (Dublin Bay prawns), shelled and*
*   coarsely chopped*
Freshly ground black pepper
A few sprigs of fresh thyme
350g/12oz dried trenette or any long dry pasta

Peel the beans and cook them in a large pan of lightly salted boiling water for 8–10 minutes or until tender. Drain.

Reserve a handful of whole beans for garnish. Put the remaining beans in a food processor with the garlic clove, 45ml/3 tbsp of the olive oil and a pinch of salt and blend for about 20 seconds. In a saucepan, heat the remaining olive oil and sauté the chopped onion. Add the bean mixture, the prawns, salt, black pepper and fresh thyme. Cook gently for about 2 minutes.

Meanwhile, cook the pasta in plenty of lightly salted boiling water until *al dente*. Drain and add to the sauce. Toss quickly in the pan over the heat to amalgamate with the sauce. Sprinkle with the reserved whole beans and black pepper. Serve immediately. Serves 4–6

Bucatini all'Amatriciana

Bucatini with Tomatoes, Onion and Pancetta

Originally a dish from the Roman countryside, this is now appreciated all over Italy and beyond. Pancetta, *onions and tomatoes are the basis of a strong rustic flavour. Bucatini, long thick spaghetti with a hole in the middle, are perfect for this sauce.*

90ml/6 tbsp extra virgin olive oil
1 onion, chopped
150g/5oz pancetta or unsmoked bacon, chopped
1 fresh hot red chilli, chopped
180ml/6fl oz (¾ cup) white wine
2 x 400g/14oz cans Italian chopped
  (crushed) tomatoes
Salt and freshly ground black pepper
450g/1lb dried bucatini
50g/2oz (½ cup) freshly grated Parmigiano
  Reggiano

In a large pan, heat the olive oil and sauté the onion for a few minutes until translucent. Add the chopped *pancetta* and the chilli and stir for 4–5 minutes until the fat of the *pancetta* becomes translucent. Add the white wine and boil to reduce before adding the tomatoes. Cover and cook over a moderate heat for about 30 minutes, stirring from time to time. Season with salt and black pepper. When the sauce is cooked, remove from the heat and set aside.

Cook the bucatini in a large pan of lightly salted boiling water until *al dente*. Drain, and add to the pan with the tomato sauce. Sprinkle with Parmesan and more black pepper and toss very well until all is amalgamated. Serve immediately. Serves 6

(see picture page 28)

Fusilli ai Peperoni

Fusilli with Red Pepper Sauce

This dish was created one night in desperation. We were completely isolated in the country and all we had were these few ingredients. It turned out to be one of the most delicious pasta dishes I have ever eaten. Remember to use only red peppers as they are sweeter and nicer than any others.

200g/7oz (14 tbsp) butter
3 red sweet peppers (capsicums), cut in strips
90ml/6 tbsp white wine
Salt
A generous amount of fresh basil leaves,
*   roughly torn*
400g/14oz fusilli, or any short dried pasta
300ml/½ pint single cream (1¼ cups light cream)
Freshly ground black pepper
110g/4oz (1 cup) freshly grated Parmigiano
*   Reggiano*

In a pan, heat the butter and sauté the peppers, adding the wine after a few minutes when the peppers have begun to soften. When tender, add some salt and the basil and cook for a further 2 minutes. Then put the contents of the pan into a food processor and blend until it has a creamy consistency.

Cook the pasta in plenty of lightly salted boiling water until *al dente*. Meanwhile, put the pepper mixture back into the pan over a gentle heat and stir in the cream, black pepper and Parmesan. Drain the pasta, transfer into the pan with the sauce, toss well and serve immediately. Serves 4–6

Making Perfect Fresh Egg Pasta

Home-made pasta has a unique lightness that the commercial dried and fresh varieties just can't equal. This is the traditional method of making pasta – it can be hard work and quite time-consuming but is immensely satisfying as well. You may be relieved to hear that you can cheat and use the food processor – your pasta may not be quite as light and elastic in texture but it is much quicker and still far better than any fresh pasta produced commercially. I have included both methods. I would not advocate the use of pasta machines that mix the flour and eggs at one end and spew various pasta shapes out the other.

400g/14oz plain flour (about 3 cups all-purpose flour) or Farina Tipo '00', plus extra for rolling out
4 eggs
A pinch of salt

These quantities will make enough pasta for 4 people. Calculate quantities at roughly 100g/3½ oz (¾ cup) of flour and 1 egg per person. In Italy the flour we use is Farina Tipo '00' which is only available outside Italy from specialist shops, but plain (all-purpose) flour is an adequate substitute. Because making fresh pasta from scratch is such a lengthy process, I often make more than I need and freeze the rest (do not defrost before cooking, but cook from frozen). The dough keeps covered in the refrigerator for 24 hours.

Mixing and kneading the traditional way:

You will need a long rolling pin and a large wooden board. Pour the flour into the middle of the board and hollow out a well in the middle. Break the eggs into it and add a pinch of salt. Stir the eggs in the middle around with your fingers, combining the yolks with the whites and gently beginning to work the mixture into the edges of the well, gradually incorporating the flour. Continue to work the flour in from the edges, keeping the mixture smooth. When the dough becomes thicker as you work in the remaining flour, start to knead it. Scrape the board of any small bits that have stuck and keep it lightly floured. Work all the flour in. The dough may start to break up a bit during kneading. Keep sprinkling with flour to prevent any stickiness. Work the dough with the heel of your hand, leaning into it; try to amalgamate the flour and egg smoothly. The kneading should take about 15–20 minutes, by which time the dough should feel quite hard and solid and no longer sticky.

Quick pasta in the food processor:

Process the eggs until well mixed. Then slowly add the flour and salt, keeping the mixture smooth. Process for about a minute or until the dough forms a ball and catches on the blade. Remove it from the machine and knead it for about 7 minutes on a lightly floured surface.

Rolling out the pasta dough:

Dust a little more flour over the board and start to roll out the dough. Roll, stretching evenly in all directions. Keep turning the dough and try to keep it circular. When it gets to about 1 cm/½ inch thickness, start rolling it away from you, folding over itself on to the rolling pin. You can feel any unevenness in the dough and can stretch it a bit by pulling at the rolling pin as you unroll. Keep repeating this routine, aiming for the thinnest sheet of dough possible. The dough will feel a bit like a hide of leather – the eggs give it a unique elasticity that will allow you to roll it very thinly, literally 1–2 mm/¹⁄₁₆ inch.

Dust the pasta very lightly with flour and fold it in sections, flouring between each fold. Using a sharp knife cut into strips. Gently unravel about 5–6 strands at a time and arrange them in nest-like shapes on lightly floured pieces of kitchen towel. Dust with a little more flour to stop sticking. At this point you can either cook the pasta immediately, freeze it (and later cook from frozen), or keep it covered at room temperature (not in the refrigerator) for up to 48 hours.

Cook the pasta in plenty of lightly salted boiling water for a couple of minutes until *al dente*, taking care not to overcook, as this will spoil the texture. Drain and serve immediately with the sauce.

A pasta machine can be used for the rolling process. These small manual machines are operated by turning a handle on the side. The sheet of pasta is pressed between the rollers, which are adjusted to make them gradually narrower. You then fold the strip back on to itself in sections of three and keep rolling it through the machine. A longer and thinner strip, that looks and feels a bit like a leather belt, emerges each time. You repeat the process until you reach the desired thickness of 1–2mm/¹⁄₁₆ inch. Leave the pasta to dry on a cloth for about 15 minutes.

For stuffed pasta *scarfioni ripieni* see page 56.

Pappardelle con Rucola, Pancetta e Gamberetti

Pappardelle with Rocket, Bacon and Prawns

*This dish is a creation of our chef Tonino Punzi who assists me in the summer
during my Cookery Weeks in Apulia. He came into the kitchen early one
morning and told me of this recipe as if he were describing a vision he had
had during the night! The guests enjoyed it immensely and it instantly became
one of the favourites in our repertoire.*

For the fresh pasta:
*400g/14oz plain flour (3 cups all-purpose
    flour) or Farina Tipo '00', plus extra for
    rolling out*
4 eggs
A pinch of salt
or:
400g/14oz dried pappardelle or fettuccine
For the sauce:
90ml/6 tbsp extra virgin olive oil
1 garlic clove, chopped
200g/7oz pancetta or smoked bacon, diced small
*25 large prawns (shrimp), uncooked, shelled
    and chopped*
90ml/6 tbsp white wine
200g/7oz ripe tomatoes, diced
Salt
100g/3½ oz rocket (arugula), roughly chopped
Freshly ground black pepper

If using fresh pasta, make it following the instructions on page 52, but do not cook until the sauce is ready.

For the sauce, heat the olive oil in a frying pan and sauté the garlic until golden. Add the bacon and prawns, then the wine and tomatoes. Season with salt and cook for about 6 minutes, adding the rocket in the last couple of minutes of cooking time.

Cook the pasta in plenty of lightly salted boiling water until *al dente*, taking care not to overcook. Drain, mix with the sauce, sprinkle with black pepper and serve immediately. Serves 4–6

Scarfioni Ripieni

Apulian Stuffed Pasta

Apulian cooking has a rustic simplicity and so does their stuffed pasta, called scarfioni, *strangely shaped with the dough only meant to seal in the very good, yet uncomplicated, filling. The dough is traditionally thick for nobody has ever learnt how to roll it thinly!*

For the filling:
500g/1lb (2 cups) ricotta cheese
3 egg yolks
50g/2oz (2 tbsp) freshly grated Parmigiano
    Reggiano or pecorino
Salt and freshly ground black pepper
A large pinch of grated nutmeg
For the pasta:
500g/1lb plain flour (about 3½ cups all-
    purpose flour) or Farina Tipo '00'
5 eggs
A pinch of salt
1 egg for sticking pasta together
For the sauce:
45ml/3 tbsp extra virgin olive oil
4 ripe tomatoes, diced
A generous amount of fresh basil leaves
Salt and freshly ground black pepper
Freshly grated Parmigiano Reggiano

Mix all the filling ingredients together in a bowl, combining well.

Make the pasta, using 5 of the eggs, and roll out as on page 53, although it need not be so thin. Use a standard kitchen drinking glass (about 7cm/3 inches across) to cut discs out of the rolled pasta.

Beat the remaining egg in a small bowl and, with a small brush, paint around the edge of each pasta disc. Put a teaspoon of filling on each pasta disc, fold in half and pinch the edges together to seal. Do make sure that they are closely sealed or they will come apart in the water. Save any leftover filling to mix with the sauce. Cook the *scarfioni* in lightly salted boiling water for 3–8 minutes, depending how thinly the pasta has been rolled. They should bob to the surface when ready. Remove carefully with a slotted spoon.

Heat the olive oil and sauté the diced tomatoes for 5 minutes. Add the basil roughly torn and season with salt and black pepper. Mix the tomato sauce with any leftover filling, and dress the *scarfioni*. Serve sprinkled with more fresh basil, Parmesan and black pepper. Serves 4–6

Stracci di Pasta con Crostacei e Zafferano

Fresh Pasta Pieces with Shellfish and Saffron

Venetians like their food to be rich and fairly complicated. This reminds them of their great past. They were not Umbrian shepherds! They were ruling the Mediterranean, conquering Europe and exploring the East. And they loved to add all the spices they had encountered in their travels to their recipes. Fish is another classic Venetian ingredient – if you happen to be in Venice don't miss the fish market in the Rialto.

1 onion, chopped into large pieces
1 celery stalk, chopped into large pieces
1 carrot, chopped into large pieces
Salt
2 litres/3½ pints (2 quarts) water
200g/7oz uncooked small prawns (small shrimp)
250g/9oz uncooked Dublin Bay or other large prawns (large shrimp)
25g/1oz (2 tbsp) unsalted butter
100g/3½ oz (¼ cup) cooked crab meat
300ml/½ pint single cream (1¼ cups light cream)
¼ tsp saffron, powdered or strands soaked in a little warm milk
350g/12oz fresh egg lasagne
Freshly ground black pepper

Make a stock by simmering the onion, celery, carrot and a pinch of salt in the water for 30 minutes. Discard the vegetables. Boil the uncooked shellfish in the stock for about 5 minutes. Remove and shell them, putting the shells back into the stock and placing the fish to one side. Simmer the stock again for about 10 minutes to reduce, then strain. Cut the shellfish into small pieces.

In a little pan heat the butter and add the cooked shellfish and crab meat. Cook and stir for about 3 minutes, then add a small ladleful of the stock. Season with salt and add the cream and saffron. Keep warm, stirring occasionally to prevent sticking.

Cut the lasagne sheets into rough pieces about 5cm/2 inches across and cook in plenty of lightly salted boiling water until *al dente*, taking care not to overcook. Drain and toss with the fish sauce, then sprinkle with black pepper and serve immediately. Serves 4

Making Perfect Gnocchi

These little Umbrian potato bites are more interesting than the standard gnocchi because of the addition of butter and Parmesan. They are simpler than they seem, but you may find that you need to practice a bit in order to perfect your technique – I suggest you devote a long rainy afternoon. The secret lies in using the right kind of potatoes. After many experiments, I find red-skinned potatoes are the best.

1kg/2lb red-skinned potatoes
Salt
25g/1oz (2 tbsp) butter
25g/1oz (¼ cup) freshly grated Parmigiano
*   Reggiano – the best Parmesan cheese*
300g/10oz plain flour (about 2 cups all-
*   purpose flour), plus some for flouring*
1 egg

Preheat the oven to 230°C/450°F/gas mark 8.

Wrap each unpeeled potato in foil and place in a roasting pan with a layer of salt scattered in the bottom to absorb humidity. Bake in the preheated oven for about 45 minutes or until cooked right through. Baking produces the best flavour – boiling the potatoes makes the gnocchi mixture too watery. When the potatoes are ready, unwrap the foil and peel off the skins. The hotter you can handle them the better – this will make it easier to work the butter in later. Push the potatoes through a potato ricer on to a big chopping board. A potato masher can also be used as the next best thing, and pushing the potato through a sieve is another alternative, if a little messier. Do try to keep the texture as light and fluffy as possible.

Spread the potato pulp over the board and then smooth in the butter using any spatula-like instrument. Do this while the potatoes are still quite hot so the butter melts in easily. Add the Parmesan and work that in the same way, or you can use your hands if the mixture is cool enough. Make a mound with the potato and next to it pour an equal amount in volume (not in weight!) of flour. Begin to amalgamate the two mounds, using your hands, and then make a well in the middle and add the egg. Make sure that the mixture is not so hot that the egg begins to cook. Knead and amalgamate all the flour, potatoes and eggs.

Lightly flour a surface and, with your hands, roll the dough into thick snake shapes about 1cm/½ inch in diameter. Sprinkle some flour over and cut into small bite-size gnocchi. Then sprinkle a little flour over the coarse side of a cheese grater and lightly press each gnocchi piece into it so the grater pattern is imprinted. This allows the gnocchi to hold the sauce. Place on a lightly floured kitchen towel and sprinkle a little extra flour over the top to prevent sticking. Leave for about 30 minutes.

Gnocchi keep for up to a day in the refrigerator, or they can be frozen and then boiled directly from frozen.

Cook the gnocchi in plenty of lightly salted boiling water for about 4 minutes. When they rise to the surface, remove with a slotted spoon and serve immediately.

Gnocchi are delicious with pesto (see page 34) or simply tossed in melted butter, with sage leaves gently fried, freshly grated Parmesan and a grinding of black pepper. They are also often served with tomato sauce (see page 44) or courgettes (see over). Serves 4

Gnocchi con Zucchine

Potato Gnocchi with Courgettes

In Italy, gnocchi are always eaten on Thursdays. With a little practice you can easily impress your friends with a Thursday dinner!

For the gnocchi:
1kg/2lb red-skinned potatoes
Salt
25g/1oz (2 tbsp) butter
25g/1 oz (¼ cup) freshly grated Parmigiano Reggiano
300g/10oz plain flour (about 2 cups all-purpose flour), plus some for flouring
1 egg
For the courgette sauce:
90ml/6 tbsp extra virgin olive oil
1 garlic clove, chopped
6 medium courgettes (zucchini), chopped small
50g/2oz (1 cup) fresh flat-leaf (continental) parsley, chopped
Salt and freshly ground black pepper
50g/2oz (½ cup) freshly grated Parmigiano Reggiano

Make the gnocchi as on page 58, but do not cook until the sauce is ready.

In a frying pan, heat the olive oil and cook the garlic and courgettes over a low heat with the lid on for about 20 minutes, until they become soft. Add the parsley, salt and black pepper.

Cook the gnocchi in plenty of lightly salted boiling water for about 4 minutes. When they rise to the surface, remove with a slotted spoon. Serve immediately, covered with the sauce and sprinkled generously with Parmesan. Serves 4–6

(see picture previous page)

Rotolo di Spinaci

Spinach and Potato Roulade

Potatoes and spinach are one of the best combinations in terms of taste and texture. My mother, who is always experimenting with food and recipes, agrees with me. This big gnocco was invented by the two of us on a rare day spent in the kitchen cooking together.

For the gnocco:
1kg/2lb red-skinned potatoes
200g/7oz plain flour (1½ cups all-purpose flour)
Salt and freshly ground black pepper
15ml/1 tbsp extra virgin olive oil
2 eggs
For the filling:
1kg/2lb spinach
25g/1oz (2 tbsp) butter
100g/3½ oz (scant ½ cup) ricotta cheese
75g/3oz (¾ cup) freshly grated Parmigiano
    Reggiano
Salt and freshly ground black pepper
A large pinch of grated nutmeg
1 egg
Preheat the oven to 230°C/450°F/gas mark 8.

Bake each unpeeled potato in foil in a roasting pan with a layer of salt scattered in the bottom for about 45 minutes or until cooked right through. When ready, unwrap the foil and peel off their skins. Push the potatoes through a potato ricer or sieve, or mash, keeping the texture light. Sift in the flour and add the salt, black pepper and olive oil. When cool enough, add the eggs and make sure everything is smoothly amalgamated, using your hands if necessary. Place the dough on a floured piece of muslin or cheesecloth and use a spatula to spread it out, aiming for a thickness of about 1cm/½ inch.

Wash the spinach carefully. Wilt it in a large covered saucepan for 2 or 3 minutes – it should cook in the little water remaining on the leaves. Drain and squeeze to remove excess water. Heat most of the butter in a large frying pan and sauté the spinach for about 4 minutes. Remove from the heat and cool. Add the ricotta, a third of the Parmesan, seasoning, nutmeg and, finally, the egg.

Spread the spinach mixture over the potato dough and roll up. Wrap the roll in the muslin or cheesecloth and secure the ends. Simmer for 40 minutes in lightly salted boiling water, then remove and unwrap the cloth. Melt the remaining butter. Slice the roulade and pour a little butter over each slice. Sprinkle the rest of the Parmesan over the top and serve immediately. Serves 4–6

Making Perfect Risotto

Risotto is a delicious speciality of northern Italian cooking, using northern ingredients such as rice, Parmigiano Reggiano and butter, and has now become popular throughout Italy. Though relatively simple to make, it can be quite difficult to perfect. It is much better cooked at home – it is such a precisely timed operation that I would never order it in a hectic restaurant.

During our Cookery Weeks, the main difficulty visitors seem to have is judging the right texture and consistency of risotto, when to stop adding stock and, more commonly, how cooked or *al dente* the rice should be. There are no specific answers to these questions. Risotto, more than any other dish, has a mind of its own and can be quite unpredictable. Being able to judge it properly comes with a mixture of practice, skill and intuition, and while there are classic steps for cooking risotto there is no foolproof formula.

Apart from top quality ingredients, risotto needs to be made with the right kind of rice: it must be Arborio, Carnaroli or Vialone Nano, which are stubby in appearance and have an almost nutty flavour when cooked. Don't even try to make it with another kind – it simply will not come out right. The only rule is to keep the desired consistency in mind.

Risotto as it is meant to be is closer to a soup than the sorry stodge that the uninitiated mistake it for – it is quite runny and wet, but creamy and velvety at the same time. It should pour from the pan into the serving dish. In the time it takes to transfer it from the pan on to the table the risotto keeps cooking, so part of the knack is being able to judge by how much you undercook it so that the transfer operations can be carried out without risk of spoiling the final texture. You should always use a shallow serving dish, not a big pasta bowl.

There are certain guidelines no matter what kind of risotto you are making. Use quite a sturdy, thick or copper-bottomed pan that will be deep enough to contain the rice – it will expand to three times its uncooked size. A thin aluminium pan is not suitable. Use a wooden spoon. The process of cooking the rice should take between 18 and 20 minutes – cooking time varies depending on the intensity of the heat and the speed with which liquid is absorbed. The order in which ingredients are added is crucial.

The flavour of a risotto is very dependent on the quality of the stock. A simple vegetable stock is described below. Alternatively, make a risotto when you have chicken or other meat stock available.

Risotto con Zafferano e Parmigiano
Risotto with Saffron and Parmesan

This saffron risotto sets a general pattern for classic risotto. It is served on its own or with ossobuco (see page 74). This is one of the few occasions in Italian cooking which combines a starter with the main course.

For the stock:
1 celery stalk, 2 carrots, 1 onion, cut in half
For the risotto:
45ml/3 tbsp extra virgin olive oil
100g/3½ oz (7 tbsp) butter
1 onion, finely chopped
350g/12oz (1½ cups) Arborio rice
360ml/12fl oz (1½ cups) white wine
1 tsp saffron, powdered or strands soaked in
*   a little warm milk*
50g/2oz (½ cup) freshly grated Parmigiano
*   Reggiano*
Salt and freshly ground black pepper

To make the stock, add the vegetables to 2.3 litres/4 pints (10 cups) of water. Simmer for 20 minutes, then strain and leave to simmer on a nearby burner while beginning the risotto. This is a standard vegetable stock that can be used in the other risotto recipes, and frozen for later use.

In a large, heavy-bottomed saucepan, heat the olive oil and half the butter. Sauté the finely chopped onion over a moderate heat for about 10 minutes. Add the rice (approximately two handfuls per person), stirring well to coat each grain with oil and toast it. This is to heat the grains to a temperature where they absorb the oil, soften and start to become translucent. After 3–4 minutes, turn the heat up a little and add the wine, allowing it to bubble and simmer away. When most of the wine has been absorbed, but the consistency is still quite liquid, add one or two ladlefuls of the hot stock, or enough to cover the rice. Stir to prevent sticking and do not allow the rice to go off the boil. The mixture should still be bubbling (looking a little like molten lava), and the grains should start to become quite plump and moist. Cook slowly on a moderate

heat, stirring continuously, adding ladlefuls of stock to keep the consistency wet and runny, almost soupy (if the risotto dries out you can't correct the consistency by adding more liquid at the end of the cooking process). As the rice absorbs the stock it releases starch which binds the risotto and makes it creamy.

After 15 minutes start testing the grains – the risotto is done when the grains are firm to the bite but the overall texture is creamy. Some people prefer the grains quite hard, so that they are even a bit chalky in the centre. Don't worry if it seems too wet and runny: the risotto will absorb all the liquid very quickly and you may even have to add another ladleful or two of stock to keep it bathed in liquid. It certainly should never be so dry that there are separate, sticky grains.

When it reaches the right consistency, remove from the heat. Add the saffron and gently fold in the rest of the butter, cut into little pieces, and the Parmesan. Season with salt and black pepper and let it stand for a minute, then pour into a serving dish, sprinkle with a little more Parmesan and black pepper, and serve immediately. Serves 4

Risotto di Mare

Seafood Risotto

*Everyone claims to have the definitive recipe for seafood risotto. I have eaten
the dish many times all over Italy, both in private homes and restaurants, and
I think my recipe is a very good one. Before beginning, read 'Making Perfect
Risotto' on page 62.*

*1.2 litres/2 pints (5 cups) fish or vegetable
stock, strained*
110g/4oz uncooked cuttlefish or squid
110g/4oz uncooked prawns (shrimp)
250g/9oz fresh mussels
250g/9oz clams
60ml/4 tbsp extra virgin olive oil
½ onion, chopped
2 garlic cloves, chopped
350g/12oz (1½ cups) Arborio rice
360ml/12fl oz (1½ cups) white wine
25g/1oz (2 tbsp) butter
*50g/2oz (1 cup) fresh flat-leaf (continental)
parsley, chopped*
Salt and freshly ground black pepper

Use white fish trimmings (bones, heads,
etc), plus the usual vegetables to make the
stock. Keep it simmering on a nearby burner.

Clean and chop up the cuttlefish. Peel the
prawns. To clean the mussels and clams soak
them in several changes of water. Scrub the
shells thoroughly and discard any which are
broken, seem abnormally heavy or float to the
top of the water. Put them in a saucepan with
about 5mm/¼ inch of water, cover and bring
to the boil. Discard any that haven't steamed
open in 5–10 minutes and remove the rest
from their shells.

In a large heavy-bottomed saucepan, heat
the olive oil and sauté the onion and garlic for
5 minutes. Add the rice, stirring well to coat

and toast all the grains. After 3–4 minutes, add
the wine and when it is absorbed start adding
the hot stock a ladleful at a time. Cook slowly
on a moderate heat, topping up with stock to
keep the consistency wet and runny, almost
soupy. After about 10 minutes, add the cuttlefish, mussels, clams and prawns. Stir to prevent
sticking and do not allow the rice to go off the
boil. After about 15 minutes of cooking the
grains of rice should be plump and yet firm to
the bite. Remove from the heat and stir in the
butter. Let it stand for a minute, then pour into
a serving dish, sprinkle with the chopped
parsley and black pepper, and serve immediately. Serves 4

Risotto con Zafferano e Fiori di Zucchine

Risotto with Saffron and Courgette Flowers

*This risotto, a favourite summer dish in Italy, involves many courgette flowers
but to good effect. Saffron adds even more yellow to this sunny, delicate risotto
which has an elegant simplicity. Before beginning, read 'Making Perfect
Risotto' on page 62.*

12 courgette (zucchini) flowers
1.2 litres/2 pints (5 cups) vegetable stock
45ml/3 tbsp extra virgin olive oil
100g/3½oz (7 tbsp) butter
1 onion, finely chopped
6 carrots, chopped
6 baby courgettes (zucchini), chopped
2 bay leaves
*350g/12oz (1½ cups) Arborio, Carnaroli or
    Vialone Nano rice*
360ml/12fl oz (1½ cups) white wine
*1 tsp saffron, powdered or strands soaked in
    a little milk*
*50g/2oz (½ cup) freshly grated Parmigiano
    Reggiano*
Salt and freshly ground black pepper

Using a sharp knife, make a fine slit down one side of each courgette flower so that it can be opened out. Pull the stalk and whole stamen out and discard. Wipe the flowers carefully and cut into strips.

Keep the stock simmering on a nearby burner.

In a large heavy-bottomed saucepan, heat the olive oil and half the butter and sauté the onion, carrots, courgettes and bay leaves for about 10 minutes. Add the rice, stirring well to coat and toast all the grains. After 3–4 minutes, add the wine and when it is absorbed start adding the hot stock a ladleful at a time. Cook slowly on a moderate heat, topping up with stock to keep the consistency wet and runny, almost soupy. Stir to prevent sticking and do not allow the rice to go off the boil. After about 15 minutes the grains of rice should be plump and yet firm to the bite. Remove from the heat and stir in the flowers cut into strips, the saffron, the rest of the butter, the Parmesan, salt and black pepper. Let it stand for a couple of minutes, then pour into a serving dish and serve immediately. Serves 4

Risotto agli Asparagi

Asparagus Risotto

The asparagus in this recipe could be replaced with other vegetables such as courgettes (zucchini) or spinach. As long as the classic steps are followed, you can use your imagination as far as vegetables are concerned, depending what is in season. The wonderful thing about risotto is that it is so versatile – it can be cold weather comfort food but equally as soothing in the summer. Before beginning, read 'Making Perfect Risotto' on page 62.

450g/1lb asparagus
1.2 litres/2 pints (5 cups) stock
45ml/3 tbsp extra virgin olive oil
100g/3½oz (7 tbsp) butter
1 onion, finely chopped
1 bay leaf
350g/12oz (1½ cups) Arborio, Carnaroli or
    Vialone Nano rice
360ml/12fl oz (1½ cups) white wine
Salt and freshly ground black pepper
50g/2oz (½ cup) freshly grated Parmigiano
    Reggiano

For this recipe you can use the tough ends of the asparagus to make the stock, setting aside the tender tips for the risotto. Keep the stock simmering on a nearby burner.

In a large, heavy-bottomed saucepan, heat the olive oil and half the butter. Sauté the finely chopped onion with the bay leaf over a moderate heat. When the onion has become translucent, after about 7 minutes, add the asparagus tips and sauté for a further 5 minutes, until the asparagus starts to soften. Keep stirring.

Add the rice, stirring well to coat and toast all the grains. After 3–4 minutes, add the white wine and when it is absorbed start adding the hot stock a ladleful at a time. Cook slowly on a moderate heat, topping up with stock to keep the consistency wet and runny, almost soupy. Stir to prevent sticking and do not allow the rice to go off the boil. After about 18 minutes the grains of rice should be plump and yet firm to the bite. Remove from the heat and stir in the rest of the butter, salt, black pepper and Parmesan. Let it stand for a minute, pour into a serving dish, sprinkle with a little more Parmesan and black pepper and serve immediately. Serves 4

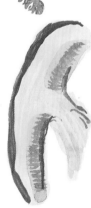
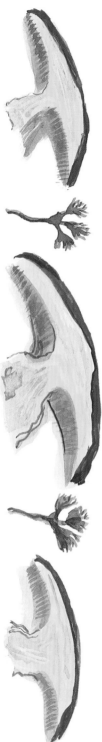

Risotto al Tartufo e Funghi Porcini

Risotto with Truffles and Mushrooms

If you are feeling very grand, I can't think of anything better than a lavish menu with plenty of truffles. If you happen to be in Italy in the autumn you will be amazed at the number of truffle dishes. This one for example is a delicious combination of truffles with ceps (porcini mushrooms). The creamy risotto binds the two aromas together in a way you will never forget. Before beginning, read 'Making Perfect Risotto' on page 62.

*25g/1oz dried porcini mushrooms, soaked in
    600ml/1 pint (2½ cups) hot water for
    about 30 minutes
600ml/1 pint (2½ cups) vegetable stock
45ml/3 tbsp extra virgin olive oil
100g/4oz (½ cup) butter
1 small onion, finely chopped
75g/3oz black or white truffle, grated
350g/12oz (1½ cups) Arborio, Carnaroli or
    Vialone Nano rice
180ml/6fl oz (¾ cup) white wine
Salt and freshly ground black pepper
75g/3oz (¾cup) freshly grated Parmigiano
    Reggiano
50g/2oz (1 cup) fresh flat-leaf (continental)
    parsley, chopped*

Drain the porcini, reserving the soaking liquid, pat dry and then chop. Keep the vegetable stock simmering on a nearby burner and add the strained porcini soaking liquid to it.

In a large, heavy-bottomed saucepan, heat the olive oil and half the butter and sauté the onion. After about 7 minutes add the truffle (but reserve a little to sprinkle over the top at the end) and porcini mushrooms. Cook for 3 minutes. Add the rice, stirring well to coat and toast all the grains. After 3–4 minutes, add the white wine and when it is absorbed start adding the hot stock a ladleful at a time. Cook slowly on a moderate heat, topping up with stock to keep the consistency wet and runny, almost soupy. Stir to prevent sticking and do not allow the rice to go off the boil. After about 18 minutes the grains of rice should be plump and yet firm to the bite. Remove from the heat and stir in the rest of the butter, the Parmesan, salt and black pepper. Let it stand for a minute, then pour into a serving dish, sprinkle the parsley and truffle over the top, and serve immediately. Serves 4

Torta di Riso e Spinaci

Rice and Spinach Flan

My classic Italian training has only allowed me to think of rice when cooked as a perfect risotto. I have never been keen on cakes made of rice, even less interested when rice is served as a bed for meat or fish. Italian cooking is still very reluctant to explore new combinations of ingredients. This rice and spinach dish is a new favourite, however, and comes from the area near Genoa, famous for the fragrance of its basil.

400g/14oz spinach
30ml/2 tbsp extra virgin olive oil
150g/5oz (10 tbsp) butter
1 onion, chopped
350g/12oz (1½ cups) Arborio rice
2 eggs, beaten
100g/3½oz (1 cup) freshly grated Parmigiano
    Reggiano – the best Parmesan cheese
180ml/6fl oz single cream (¾ cup light cream)
Salt and freshly ground black pepper
A large pinch of grated nutmeg
A generous amount of fresh basil leaves,
    roughly torn

Preheat the oven to 180°C/350°F/gas mark 4.

Wash the spinach carefully and drain. Wilt it in a large saucepan for 2 or 3 minutes – is should cook in the little water remaining on the leaves, but if there is any danger of burning, add a spoonful or two of additional water. Drain and squeeze to remove excess water. Heat the oil and half the butter in a frying pan and sauté the spinach and onion. Boil the rice in salted water for only 8 minutes; drain.

In a large bowl mix the rice with the remaining butter, the beaten eggs, Parmesan, spinach and cream. Add salt, black pepper, nutmeg and, finally, the fresh basil. Oil a glass or terracotta oven-proof dish, about 6cm/2 inches deep, and pour in the rice mixture. Cook in the preheated oven for 15 minutes. Serve on its own or with a light tomato sauce (see page 90). Serves 4

Secondi piatti. *Meat and fish are important in Italian cooking, but less central to a style of eating which relies so heavily on good vegetables and other staples. Meat like good beef or veal is really only an important part of northern Italian food, while southern regions have traditionally relied on fish. In northern pastures, cattle are raised for veal as well as for milk to make famous cheeses like Parmigiano Reggiano. Every farmer keeps a pig or two to turn into cured hams and salami in the winter months, while chicken, rabbit and game add variety. South of Tuscany, lamb assumes the central role typical of all Mediterranean cuisines, and is present at nearly every meal. Whenever I drive into the Apulian south, I am amazed at the change in the landscape, as flat terrain covered with olive trees stretches to meet the blue of the sea. This is the land where simple fish is served flavoured with garlic, chillies and oregano, dressed with olive oil.*

Involtini al Sugo

Stuffed Veal Escalopes in Tomato Sauce

What could be more Apulian than this veal dish? Rolled and stuffed, it features all the classic southern ingredients. This is more tomato sauce than you will need for the veal – use about a quarter for the veal and the rest to dress a dish of pasta.

4 veal escalopes (veal cutlets), cut in half
Salt
3 garlic cloves, finely chopped
50g/2oz (1 cup) fresh flat-leaf (continental) parsley, chopped
8 celery leaves, chopped
About 20 pine nuts
About 20 sultanas (golden raisins)
180ml/6fl oz (¾ cup) extra virgin olive oil
½ onion, chopped
90ml/6 tbsp white wine
For the tomato sauce:
60ml/4 tbsp extra virgin olive oil
½ onion, finely chopped
2 fresh hot red chillies, finely chopped
2 x 400g/14oz cans chopped (crushed) tomatoes
Fresh basil leaves, roughly torn
Fresh flat-leaf (continental) parsley, chopped
Salt and freshly ground black pepper

To make the tomato sauce, heat the olive oil and sauté the onion and chillies for about 4 minutes. When the onion becomes translucent, add the chopped tomatoes and cook for a further 20 minutes. Remove from the heat. Add the basil and parsley and season with salt and black pepper. Set aside.

Spread out the slices of veal on a flat surface. Sprinkle salt, garlic, parsley (saving half for garnish), celery leaves, pine nuts and sultanas on each slice of meat. Roll up and secure each with a wooden toothpick. Heat the olive oil in a frying pan and sauté the onion. When translucent, add the veal rolls and cook for about 5 minutes, browning lightly on all sides. Add the wine and the tomato sauce. Cover and leave to cook for 10 minutes.

Check the seasoning. Serve the veal rolls covered with the sauce and garnished with the reserved parsley, with green beans to accompany. Serves 4

Ossobuco

Veal Braised in White Wine

There are many different stories behind the famous northern Italian dish of ossobuco. Some say that the overworked Milanese people adopted this recipe, which is usually served with a perfect saffron risotto, in order to save time and get back to work. Others say that the combination of meat and rice, which is not at all usual in Italy, dates back to when the Austrians ruled Milan in the eighteenth and nineteenth centuries. Today it is cooked in every northern home. This dish can only be made with the best quality shin of veal, with marrow in the bone.

Flour to dust the meat
Salt and freshly ground black pepper
6 thick slices of shin of veal (crosscuts of veal hind shank), with the marrow
50g/2oz (4 tbsp) butter
300ml/½ pint (1¼ cups) dry white wine
300g/11oz (1¼ cups) chopped tomatoes
600ml/1 pint (2½ cups) vegetable stock (see page 63)
For the gremolata sauce:
6 tbsp chopped fresh flat-leaf (continental) parsley
1 tbsp finely chopped lemon zest
1 garlic clove, crushed

Season some flour with salt and black pepper and dust the veal lightly. Melt the butter in a heavy, lidded casserole and sauté the veal pieces gently until golden on both sides. Add the wine and simmer for about 15 minutes. Add the tomatoes and about half the stock and season with salt and black pepper. Cover and cook over a low heat for a further 1 hours, stirring occasionally and adding more stock if it begins to dry out.

Meanwhile, prepare the *gremolata* by mixing the parsley, lemon zest and garlic together. About 10 minutes before serving, place a spoonful of *gremolata* on each piece of veal and continue to simmer gently. Serve each *ossobuco* with some of the thick sauce and a saffron risotto (see page 62). The marrow from each slice of veal, eaten with the rice, is a great delicacy. Serves 6

Polpettine in Salsa di Pomodoro

Meatballs in Tomato Sauce

Meatballs made with fresh ingredients are delicious. Here the addition of tomato sauce creates an even more substantial dish.

100g/3½oz (scant ½ cup) fresh ricotta cheese
100g/3½oz (1 cup) Emmenthal cheese,
  roughly chopped or grated
100g/3½oz very lean minced pork (½ cup
  very lean ground pork)
150g/5oz minced veal (⅔ cup ground veal)
1 egg
Salt and freshly ground black pepper
Sunflower oil for frying
For the tomato sauce:
6 fresh ripe tomatoes, or 1 x 400g/14oz can
  chopped (crushed) tomatoes
60ml/4 tbsp extra virgin olive oil
½ onion, finely chopped
Fresh basil leaves, roughly torn
Salt and freshly ground black pepper

To make the tomato sauce, first blanch the fresh tomatoes. Make a cross with a sharp knife at the bottom of each tomato, just to split the skin. Plunge the tomatoes into boiling water for 1 minute, or until the cross at the base starts to open up. Remove with a slotted spoon and peel off the skin, which should come away easily with a sharp knife. Remove core and seeds and chop the flesh. Heat the olive oil and sauté the onion for about 4 minutes. When the onion becomes translucent, add the chopped tomatoes and cook for 10 minutes, or 20 minutes for canned tomatoes. Remove from the heat. Add the basil and season with salt and black pepper. Keep warm until the meatballs are ready.

Mix the cheeses, the meats and the egg together. Season with salt and black pepper and shape into little balls the size of a cherry. Heat sunflower oil in a frying pan. When the oil is very hot, add the meatballs in batches, frying for about 2–3 minutes until crisp. Remove and drain on kitchen paper. Serve with the tomato sauce on the side. Serves 4

Petto di Vitello con Uva e Melograno

Veal Noisettes with Grapes and Pomegranates

This is an Umbrian recipe, full of flavour, slightly more refined than many other country dishes. It looks very pretty and tastes delicious.

4 noisettes of veal about 4cm/1½ inches thick
4 slices of pancetta *or unsmoked bacon*
30 juniper berries
15 black pepper grains
40g/1½ oz (3 tbsp) butter
90ml/3fl oz (6 tbsp) sparkling dry white wine
12 sweet white grapes, cut in half
Seeds of ½ pomegranate
Salt and freshly ground black pepper

Pound the juniper berries and black pepper and set aside. Wrap each piece of meat with a slice of *pancetta* and secure tightly with cotton string. Then coat the edges of each parcel with the crushed berries.

Melt the butter in a large frying pan, making sure that it doesn't burn. As soon as the butter is melted arrange the meat in the pan and cook on each side for about 3 minutes or until the meat turns golden. Pour the white wine into the pan together with the grapes and the pomegranate seeds. Season with salt and black pepper. Simmer over a moderate heat for another 5 minutes or so to allow the sauce to reduce. Arrange the noisettes in a warm serving dish and surround with the sauce. Serve immediately, accompanied with mashed potatoes with herbs (see page 111). Serves 4

Costolette d'Agnello 'Lo Spagnulo'
Lamb Cutlets 'Lo Spagnulo' Style

When you find an Italian dish stuffed or in layers you can rest assured that it comes from Apulia. These lamb cutlets with pepper sauce are popular eaten very hot and served with an accompanying salad.

4-6 lamb cutlets (lamb rib chops), at least
*   1cm/½ inch thick*
75g/3oz (¾ cup) freshly grated Parmesan
75g/3oz (6 tbsp) ricotta cheese
180ml/6fl oz single cream (¾ cup light cream)
200g/7oz cooked ham, cut into slices
2 fresh tomatoes, sliced
2 eggs
Salt
110g/4oz (1 cup) fine dry breadcrumbs
Sunflower oil for frying
For the pepper sauce:
90ml/6 tbsp extra virgin olive oil
1 onion, chopped
1 garlic clove
A bunch of flat-leaf (continental) parsley, chopped
4 yellow sweet peppers (capsicums), diced
180ml/6fl oz (¾ cup) white wine
2 fresh tomatoes, chopped
Salt and freshly ground pepper
A few fresh basil leaves

Preheat the oven to 140°C/275°F/gas mark 1.

Mix together the Parmesan, ricotta and cream. Make a deep incision into the side of the meat of each of the cutlets. Pack the cutlets with the cheese mixture, a slice of ham and a small slice of tomato. Seal the sides, pressing the edges together. Whisk the eggs and add a pinch of salt. Dip the cutlets in the egg, then coat with the breadcrumbs. Heat the sunflower oil and fry the cutlets for about 5 minutes on each side. Keep warm.

To make the pepper sauce, heat the olive oil and sauté the onion until soft, adding the peeled garlic and parsley. When golden, add the peppers and stir. Pour in the wine and, when evaporated, add the tomatoes and salt and black pepper. Remove the garlic. Cook for 15 minutes, stirring from time to time.

Serve the cutlets with the sauce on the side, sprinkled with basil leaves. Serves 4–6

Pollo Farcito con le Noci

Stuffed Chicken with Walnuts

Chicken is one of the most versatile of all ingredients. This recipe comes from the foggy countryside near Milan where they like their dishes to be rather opulent.

10 walnuts, shelled and coarsely chopped
1 apple, chopped in small pieces
100g/3½oz Italian luganega sausage, or the best Cumberland or pure pork sausage, skinned and crumbled
16 stoned prunes, plumped up in warm water if necessary
A handful of sultanas (golden raisins), plumped up in warm water
Salt and freshly ground pepper
1 free-range chicken, weighing about 1.5 kg/3lb
50g/2oz (4 tbsp) butter
180 ml/6fl oz (¾ cup) dry white wine

Make the stuffing by mixing together the walnuts, apple, crumbled sausage, half the pitted prunes and half the sultanas. Season with salt and black pepper. Wipe the chicken inside and out and stuff the cavity with the walnut mixture. Secure the chicken at both ends with cotton string.

Melt the butter in a heavy, lidded casserole and add the chicken, browning on all sides. Add the remaining pitted prunes and sultanas and the white wine and sprinkle with salt and black pepper. Cook with the lid on for about 1 hour over a moderate heat, turning the chicken from time to time.

When cooked, carve the chicken into pieces, spoon out the stuffing and arrange on a serving dish with the sauce, fruit and stuffing on top. Serves 4–6

Maialino con le Verze

Pork and Red Cabbage

A northern Italian recipe where the presence of red cabbage might suggest an Austrian influence. Northern Italians like their food to be rich and full of flavour. This is ideal winter food.

1 medium red cabbage
60g/2oz (4 tbsp) butter
1kg/2lb boned piece of pork
40g/1½oz (3 heaped tbsp) sugar
360ml/12fl oz (1½ cups) red wine
Salt and freshly ground black pepper

In a casserole melt the butter and add the pork. Brown the meat on all sides. Add the sugar and red wine, season with salt and black pepper and bring to the boil. Put the lid on the casserole and simmer over a low heat for about 1 hour or until the meat is almost tender.

Wash the cabbage, remove the core and then cut into thin strips. Add the chopped cabbage to the casserole and cook for a further 30 minutes or until the meat is cooked. Check the seasoning. Cut the pork into slices of about 1cm/½ inch thickness and arrange on a serving dish surrounded by the red cabbage. Serves 4–6

Agnello e Patate al Forno
Apulian-Style Roast Lamb with Potatoes

An Apulian version of English shepherd's pie. Here the meat is cooked together with the potatoes, tomatoes, oregano and rosemary, and it certainly has a different flavour.

1kg/2lb potatoes
1kg/2lb lean lamb
50g/2oz (1 heaped cup) fresh breadcrumbs
 or crumbled bread
50g/2oz (½ cup) freshly grated Parmigiano
 Reggiano – the best Parmesan cheese
2 garlic cloves, chopped
50g/2oz (1 cup) fresh flat-leaf (continental)
 parsley, chopped
A few sprigs of fresh rosemary and oregano,
 chopped
Freshly ground black pepper
180ml/6fl oz (¾ cup) extra virgin olive oil
10 ripe tomatoes, chopped
About 180ml/6fl oz (¾ cup) white wine
About 180ml/6fl oz (¾ cup) water
Salt

Preheat the oven to 200°C/400°F/gas mark 6.

Wash and peel the potatoes. Cut large ones into eight pieces and smaller ones into quarters, trying to try keep them all the same size. Cut the lamb into cubes about the same size as the potatoes. Mix the breadcrumbs, Parmesan, garlic, parsley, rosemary, oregano and black pepper together in a bowl.

Spoon about 45ml/3 tbsp of olive oil over the bottom of a large roasting pan or oven dish and add a layer of potatoes. Spread some of the herb mixture on top and then add a layer of lamb. Salt each layer. Add layers of chopped tomatoes, more potatoes, then meat, and finish with the herb mixture. Drizzle with the remaining olive oil, and add enough wine and water to cover the first layer of potatoes. Season with salt and more rosemary. Cook in the oven for 1–1½ hours until the potatoes are tender. Serves 6

(see picture opposite)

Pollo con Olive, Aglio e Rosmarino

Chicken with Olives, Garlic and Rosemary

A very simple yet delicious chicken recipe, full of good flavours, and like many simple dishes, if properly made, it is one of the best.

60ml/4 tbsp extra virgin olive oil
2 onions, roughly chopped
1 free-range chicken, weighing about 1.8kg/4lb,
*   cut into 6 pieces*
120ml/4fl oz (½ cup) white wine
2 sprigs of fresh rosemary, chopped
100g/3½oz (⅔ cup) black olives, pitted
2 garlic cloves, chopped
15ml/1 tbsp red wine vinegar
Salt and freshly ground black pepper

Heat the olive oil in a heavy casserole. Add the onions and, when they begin to soften, add the chicken pieces, turning to coat in the olive oil. They should be browned lightly on both sides after about 10 minutes. Add the white wine. Turn the heat down, cover and simmer the chicken for about 45 minutes. The meat should be tender and juicy.

About 5 minutes before the end of cooking, remove the lid, turn up the heat and add the chopped rosemary, olives, garlic and vinegar. Season with salt and black pepper. Stir well and serve very hot. Serves 6

Pollo all'Orvietana

Chicken Orvieto Style

*This is rustic Umbrian cooking at its best, with some of the potatoes actually
cooked inside the chicken.*

*1 free range chicken, weighing about 1.5kg/3lb,
   with giblets
Vinegar
90ml/6 tbsp extra virgin olive oil
A bunch each of fresh rosemary and herb
   fennel, chopped
30 black olives
3 potatoes, diced
Salt and freshly ground black pepper
4 garlic cloves, 2 peeled and chopped, 2 unpeeled
180ml/6fl oz (¾ cup) white wine*

Preheat the oven to 200°C/400°F/gas mark 6.

Remove the giblets from the chicken. Clean the liver of any discoloured patches, wash in cold water several times and then give it a final rinse of vinegar. Chop the heart and liver into small pieces. In a pan, heat half the olive oil and sauté the chopped giblets, the rosemary and fennel, 20 of the black olives, the potatoes and 2 cloves of chopped garlic for 5 minutes. Season with salt and black pepper, add half the white wine and cook for another 5 minutes until the liver is done. Salt the chicken inside and out and loosely stuff it with the sautéed mixture. Secure the chicken with cotton string or skewers. Season with more salt and black pepper. Place the chicken, breast down, in a roasting pan and add the rest of the olive oil, wine and black olives and the unpeeled cloves of garlic, slightly crushed, together with any left-over stuffing. Cook in the preheated oven for 1 hour. Carve the chicken and serve on a dish with stuffing on the side and the sauce poured over.

Serves 6

Anatra con Vin Santo

Duck in Sweet Wine

I love Vin Santo. Amber in colour and sweetish with a slightly sherry-like character, it reminds me of Tuscany where I used to spend a lot of time when I was younger. In Tuscan cooking this delightful sweet wine is used both in meat courses and for desserts. Here it adds flavour to the duck and creates an excellent sauce.

180ml/6fl oz (¾ cup) extra virgin olive oil
2 onions, chopped
1 celery stalk, chopped
2 carrots, chopped
150g/5oz fatty Parma ham (prosciutto),
    chopped
6 fresh sage leaves, chopped
1 duck, weighing 1.4kg/3lb, cut into 4 pieces,
    with the liver
Salt and freshly ground black pepper
900ml/1½ pints (3¾ cups) Vin Santo or
    medium dry sherry

In a large frying pan heat the olive oil and sauté all the vegetables with the Parma ham and sage over a moderate heat. When the vegetables become translucent, add the pieces of duck, turning them until they brown lightly on each side. Season with salt and black pepper, then add half of the Vin Santo. Cover and leave to cook for about 15 minutes.

Stir and add the rest of the wine and the washed and chopped duck liver. Cook for another hour, stirring from time to time and adding a little water if it begins to dry out at all. The sauce should be reasonably thick.

When the duck is cooked remove the pieces from the sauce and leave to rest in a warm oven. Allow the sauce to cool. After about 15 minutes the fat will come to the surface and you can skim it off with a spoon. Gently reheat the sauce and pour over the duck before serving. Serves 4

Piccioni in Salmi

Pigeons in Red Wine Sauce

Pigeons are popular all over Umbria and Tuscany. Their meat is surprisingly tender and juicy, and it has a delicious strong taste. In Umbria the sauce from the meat is served over pasta, either before the main course or the following day.

4 pigeons (squabs)
Vinegar
60ml/4 tbsp extra virgin olive oil
2 celery stalks, chopped
2 onions, chopped
2 carrots, chopped
½ lemon
1 garlic clove, chopped
Fresh sage and rosemary, chopped
1 bay leaf
8 juniper berries
4 cloves
360ml/12fl oz (1½ cups) red wine
Salt and freshly ground black pepper
4 slices of toasted country bread

Clean the pigeons inside and out, wash them in cold water and rinse with vinegar. Heat the olive oil in a heavy casserole and sauté the celery, onions, carrots, lemon half, garlic, herbs and spices for about 10 minutes, stirring occasionally. Add the pigeons and the red wine and cook with the lid on for about 40 minutes.

Remove the pigeons and cut each in half. Remove the lemon and the bay leaf and then finely chop or briefly work the ingredients left in the pan in a food processor until they reach a creamy consistency. Season with salt and black pepper. Arrange a slice of toasted bread on each plate, cover with two pieces of pigeon and pour the sauce over. Serves 4

Coniglio con Pinoli ed Uvetta

Rabbit with Pine Nuts and Sultanas

My mother is very keen on rabbit and this is an old family recipe. The pine nuts and sultanas would suggest some sort of Sicilian influence. My mother's family has, however, lived in Milan for over 200 years.

*1 rabbit, weighing 1.8kg/4lb, cut in 8-10
    pieces, with the liver
180ml/6fl oz (¾ cup) extra virgin olive oil
4 sprigs of fresh rosemary
Salt and freshly ground black pepper
180ml/6fl oz (¾ cup) white wine
6 medium potatoes, peeled and cut in slices
    about 1cm/½ inch thick
30ml/2 tbsp balsamic vinegar
90ml/6 tbsp dry Marsala or medium dry sherry
A handful of sultanas (golden raisins),
    plumped up in warm water for ½ hour
A handful of pine nuts*

Preheat the oven to 180°C/350°F/gas mark 4.

Wash the rabbit pieces, pat dry and marinate in half the olive oil with 2 sprigs of rosemary, salt, black pepper and the white wine for at least 6 hours in a cool place.

Heat the remaining olive oil in a large pan, add the sliced potatoes and remaining rosemary sprigs and sprinkle with salt. Place the rabbit pieces and the marinade in a large cast iron pan, covered with a lid. Put both pans in the preheated oven. After about 30 minutes when the rabbit starts to brown, remove the rabbit. Leave the potatoes to continue cooking for another 30 minutes.

Remove the rabbit from its pan and keep warm. Put the pan on a moderate heat and cook the sauce, stirring from time to time, until it has reduced. With a fork mash the liver into the sauce and, when it starts to change colour, add the balsamic vinegar and Marsala. Allow to simmer and reduce for a few minutes. Keep stirring, making sure the sauce does not stick. Then add the sultanas and pine nuts and cook for a further 5 minutes.

Return the pieces of rabbit to the sauce. Add the potatoes and oil from their oven dish. Stir well. Cook together in the oven for another 30 minutes, until the rabbit and potatoes are tender. Serve immediately. Serves 4–6

Tonno con Pomodorini, Basilico ed Origano

Tuna with Cherry Tomatoes, Basil and Oregano

This is an Apulian dish using all the classic southern ingredients. It looks great and tastes even better.

1 slice of fresh tuna, weighing 500g/1lb
Salt and freshly ground black pepper
30ml/2 tbsp extra virgin olive oil
1 garlic clove, chopped
10-15 cherry tomatoes, cut in half
Fresh oregano
A few fresh basil leaves

Tie the tuna slice with fine string so that it retains its shape. Season on both sides with salt and black pepper. Heat the olive oil in a frying pan and sauté the garlic briefly. When the pan is very hot, add the tuna and cook for about 5–6 minutes on each side. Add the cherry tomatoes and cook for another 5 minutes. Remove from the heat. Season with salt, black pepper, oregano and basil leaves. Remove the string and divide the fish into four. Serve with a fresh mixed salad. Serves 4

Pesce in Crosta di Sale con Pomodorini al Vapore

Fresh Fish in Salt Crust with Steamed Cherry Tomatoes

This idea of cooking the fish under a mountain of salt never appealed greatly to me. But once I tried it I found the fish remains moist and juicy. The simple fish combines well with the delicate cherry tomato sauce.

1kg/2lb (7 cups) coarse sea salt
2 egg whites
180ml/6fl oz (¾ cup) water
2 trout or seabass, weighing about 400g/
    14oz each, cleaned
For the steamed cherry tomatoes:
300g/12oz cherry tomatoes, red and sweet
10 fresh basil leaves
45ml/3 tbsp extra virgin olive oil
Preheat the oven to 200°C/400°F/gas mark 6.

Mix the sea salt with the egg whites and water. Place the fish in a baking tray or oven dish and cover evenly with the salt mixture. Cook in the preheated oven for about 20 minutes or until the crust is golden.

Meanwhile, prepare the cherry tomatoes. Put the tomatoes, basil and olive oil in a bain-marie or heat-proof glass bowl set on a pan of boiling water. Cook for about 25 minutes until the tomatoes are nearly falling apart.

When the fish is ready, break the salt crust, lift the fish out and remove all the salt and skin. Fillet the fish and serve with the cherry tomatoes on the side. Serves 4

Involtini di Pesce Spada

Rolled Swordfish

This very refreshing fish recipe is a revelation, with a sunny, summer flavour. The ingredients are all easy to find and even if you make it in the winter, it will put you in a summery mood.

2 lemons
4 spring onions (scallions), finely chopped
A small bunch of fresh mint, chopped
200g/7oz canned tuna in olive oil, drained

90ml/6 tbsp olive oil
Salt and freshly ground black pepper
6 thin slices of swordfish
Small bunch flat-leaf (continental) parsley

Thinly pare the zest from one of the lemons. Squeeze the juice from both lemons and set aside. Chop the lemon zest finely and mix with the spring onions, mint, tuna, 30ml/ 2 tbsp olive oil, salt and black pepper. Spread the mixture on the slices of swordfish. Roll up the slices and secure with fine cotton string or wooden toothpicks.

Grill the swordfish rolls under a very hot grill (broiler), or on a griddle or ridged grill pan, for at least 6 minutes on each side. Arrange on a flat dish and dress with the rest of the olive oil, the lemon juice and chopped parsley. Serves 6

Gamberetti con le Fave

Broad Bean and Prawn Salad

When in season, young fresh broad beans are delicious. This unusual combination comes once again from Apulia where, although they are attached to their cooking traditions, they also like to experiment. I sometimes serve this dish as an antipasto.

For the salad:
*300g/11oz (2 cups) young broad (fava)
  beans, shelled*
2 leeks
2 carrots
1 red onion, finely chopped
*550g/1¼ lb freshly cooked prawns (large
  shrimp), peeled*
For the dressing:
90ml/6 tbsp extra virgin olive oil
1 garlic clove, finely chopped
15ml/1 tbsp white wine vinegar
5ml/1 tsp Dijon mustard
Juice of ½ lemon
Salt and freshly ground black pepper

Cook the broad beans in boiling water for no more than 6 minutes, drain and put to one side. Remove most of the green from the washed leeks, and cut into strips lengthways. Cut the peeled carrots into strips lengthways. Blanch the vegetable strips for 4 minutes, then put in a bowl with the beans and the red onion. Add the prawns and mix together with the vegetables.

Combine all the dressing ingredients and pour over the salad just before serving. Serve warm or cold. Serves 6 as an antipasto, 4 as a main course

Spigola con Arancio e Carciofi

Fillets of Seabass or Trout with Oranges and Artichokes

This delightful fresh salad of fish with oranges and artichokes comes from Antonio Bondi, the chef who works with me in Umbria during our Cookery Weeks. I have recently discovered that in Apulia they have a similar recipe using tangerines and fresh limes. This dish can be served at room temperature or slightly chilled in summer.

400g/14oz seabass or trout fillets
Salt and freshly ground black pepper
100g/3½oz white celery
2 tender baby globe artichokes
2 blood oranges, peeled and cut in segments
75ml/5 tbsp extra virgin olive oil
Juice of 1 lemon

Wash the fish and season with salt and black pepper. Steam over a large pan of boiling water for 10 minutes. Cool and skin the fish. Place on the bottom of a flat serving dish.

Chop the celery diagonally in pieces of about 3cm/1¼ inches. Wash the artichokes, remove the outer leaves and cut off the tips and the stalk at the base. Remove any trace of the choke, leaving only the very tender hearts. Cut into quarters.

Cover the fish with layers of celery, orange segments and slivers of raw artichoke hearts. Just before serving, dress with the olive oil, lemon juice, salt and black pepper, and toss gently. Serves 4

Verdure. Italians are passionate about vegetables. There are regional variations in what the local country markets display – beans and spinach are found everywhere, but further south you see increasing mounds of aubergines and in the far south chillies and more fiery variations of herbs like rucola *(rocket or arugula). Many kinds of tomato are available, and I tend to choose the round cherry tomatoes most often for their sweetness. Vegetables are not merely an accompaniment to meat and fish. Many vegetable dishes can stand on their own, and three together make a hearty meal:* fave e cicoria *could be served followed by a dish of stuffed vegetables, baked onions and a salad of mixed leaves. There is always a certain simplicity in Italian vegetable cooking, based on the use of very fresh, high quality ingredients and a small number of flavours combined together in any one dish. Simply anointed with good olive oil, they are frequently the star of the show.*

Asparagi Al Forno

Baked Asparagus

Asparagus is very dear to the Italians, especially in the north where they like to serve it with butter and Parmesan and a fried egg on the side. This more rustic Umbrian version with olive oil is equally delicious and probably has more flavour.

800g/1½lb white or green asparagus
Salt and freshly ground black pepper
90ml/6 tbsp extra virgin olive oil
50g/2oz (½ cup) freshly grated Parmigiano
Reggiano - the best Parmesan cheese

Preheat the oven to 180°C/350°F/gas mark 4.

Clean the asparagus and trim off the woody ends of the stalks if necessary. Place the asparagus in a pan of lightly salted boiling water and cook for about 8 minutes over a moderate heat. The water should be simmering, not boiling.

Drain with a slotted spoon and lay the asparagus in a buttered terracotta dish. Season with a pinch of salt and black pepper. Drizzle the olive oil over the top and sprinkle with Parmesan. Bake in the preheated oven for about 6–7 minutes, until lightly golden.
Serves 4

Involtini di Peperoni
Rolled Red Peppers

*The country markets of Italy are always full of sweet peppers. Italians use red
or yellow peppers in their cooking, never the green variety, which is bitter.
Here peppers are stuffed with the strong flavours of garlic and capers.*

3 ripe red tomatoes
*300g/10oz buffalo mozzarella cheese, cut
    into cubes*
4 red sweet peppers (capsicums)
*15ml/1 tbsp chopped fresh flat-leaf
    (continental) parsley*
10 black olives, pitted and chopped
30ml/2 tbsp capers, rinsed and chopped
3 tbsp freshly grated Parmigiano Reggiano
3 garlic cloves, chopped
Salt and freshly ground black pepper
*½ tsp dried oregano, or a handful of fresh
    basil leaves, roughly torn*
Extra virgin olive oil for drizzling

Preheat the oven to 190°C/375°F/gas mark 5.

Make a cross with a sharp knife at the base
of each tomato, just to split the skin. Plunge
the tomatoes into boiling water for 1 minute,
or until the cross at the base starts to open up.
Remove with a slotted spoon and peel off the
skin, which should come away easily with a
sharp knife. Remove core and seeds and chop
the flesh. Put the chopped tomatoes and
mozzarella in a sieve to drain off any excess
liquid.

Cut the peppers in half lengthways and
remove the seeds. Bake on a unoiled baking
tray for 20–30 minutes until they start to
collapse and the skins blacken. Transfer to a
bowl and cover with foil to trap moisture.
Leave for about 10 minutes until the skin
loosens. Peel the peppers and remove seeds.

Reserve the liquid that has collected at the
bottom of the bowl.

Keep back 3 tbsp of chopped tomatoes
and a little fresh parsley. Mix together the rest
of the tomatoes and parsley with the mozzarella, black olives, capers, Parmesan, garlic, salt
and black pepper. Use to fill the pepper halves.
As you fill the peppers roll them up and place
in a terracotta oven dish. Mix together the
remaining tomatoes and parsley with the
oregano or basil, sprinkle over the pepper
rolls, and pour over the liquid reserved from
peeling the peppers. Drizzle with olive oil and
bake in the preheated oven for 15 minutes or
until golden and bubbling. Serve warm with
plenty of country bread. Serves 4

Peperoni Arrosto con Acciughe

Roast Peppers with Anchovies

Roasting peppers is routine in any Italian kitchen and the soft sweet flesh can also be used for dressing pasta or as a topping for bruschetta. You can keep roasted peppers in the refrigerator for 2 or 3 days. This is a classic pepper dish, known all over Italy.

4 red or yellow sweet peppers (capsicums)
8 canned anchovies, drained and chopped
2 garlic cloves, crushed
180ml/6fl oz (¾ cup) extra virgin olive oil
Salt and freshly ground black pepper

Preheat the oven to 190°C/375°F/gas mark 5.

Put the peppers on an unoiled baking tray and roast them in the oven for 20–30 minutes until they start to collapse and the skins blacken. Transfer to a bowl and cover with foil to trap moisture. Leave for about 10 minutes until the skin loosens. Peel the peppers, cut open and remove the stem and seeds. Cut the flesh into pieces and put in a serving dish.

Make the dressing by mixing the anchovies, garlic, olive oil and salt and black pepper together until creamy in consistency. Pour over the peppers and serve. Serves 4

Tiella di Verdure al Forno
Apulian Layered Vegetables

This is always voted the most popular dish during our Cookery Weeks in Apulia. Tonino, our chef, and I have developed, adapted and finally perfected this typically southern recipe.

4 courgettes (zucchini), sliced lengthways
3 aubergines (eggplants), sliced lengthways
Flour for dusting
Sunflower oil for deep frying
450g/1lb Swiss chard (silver beet), white parts only, cut into pieces
450g/1lb certosa fresca *or other melting cheese, e.g. Gruyère, Emmental or a combination, thinly sliced*
300g/10½oz pancetta, *cooked ham or unsmoked bacon, in slices*
100g/3½oz (1 cup) freshly grated Parmigiano Reggiano - the best Parmesan cheese
Salt and freshly ground black pepper

Preheat the oven to 200°C/400°F/gas mark 6.

Dust the sliced courgettes and aubergines with flour and deep fry in plenty of oil until golden. Remove with a slotted spoon and drain on kitchen paper. Cook the Swiss chard in salted boiling water for 8 minutes or until tender and then drain.

In a large terracotta or other oven-proof dish, make alternate layers of courgettes, melting cheese, *pancetta*, aubergines and Swiss chard, in that order, sprinkling Parmesan, salt and black pepper between each layer. Finish with a thick layer of melting cheese and Parmesan. Bake for 20–30 minutes. Serves 6

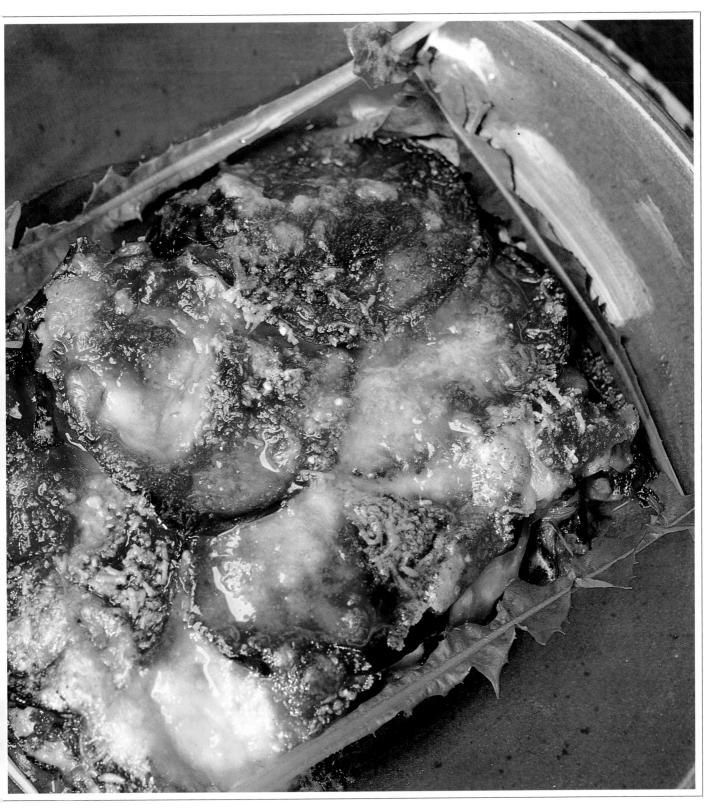

Terrina Bianca e Verde

White and Green Asparagus and Broad Bean Terrine

Young, tender asparagus is a speciality of the Veneto region. Here, combined with cream and fresh ricotta, they are especially delicate in flavour. The final dish looks elaborate but it is in fact very simple to make.

450g/1lb shelled fresh broad beans (2½–3 cups shelled fresh fava beans)
12 large asparagus spears, white or green
60ml/4 tbsp single (light) cream
1 egg
Salt and freshly ground black pepper
100g/3½oz (1 cup) freshly grated Parmigiano Reggiano
400g/14oz (1¼ cups) fresh ricotta cheese
15ml/1 tbsp extra virgin olive oil
25g/1oz (2 tbsp) butter, melted

Preheat the oven to 200°C/400°F/gas mark 6.

Line a shallow glass or terracotta rectangular mould, of 900ml/1½ pint (1 quart) capacity, with foil. Remove and discard the tough outer skins of the beans and cook them in lightly salted boiling water for 7–10 minutes, until tender. Drain and set aside to cool. Break the tough ends off the asparagus and discard. Simmer the spears gently in a little lightly salted water for 5 minutes or until tender. Drain and cut in half lengthways.

Keep a few beans aside for decoration, and purée the rest in a food processor together with the cream, egg, salt, black pepper and 4 tbsp of Parmesan. Mix the ricotta with the olive oil and some salt and black pepper.

Cover the bottom of the mould with half of the asparagus, arranging it in one layer, cut side up. Add a layer of half of the broad bean purée, then a layer of half of the ricotta. Repeat these layers, sprinkling with more salt and black pepper as you go. Cover with foil and set the mould in a bain-marie, or roasting pan half filled with warm water. Cook in the oven for 1 hour. Remove from the oven and lift the mould out of the bain-marie. Leave to cool at room temperature.

Turn out the terrine and remove the foil. Decorate with the reserved broad beans. Cut into slices and dress with melted butter, more black pepper and the rest of the Parmesan. Serves 6

Crocchette di Carciofi
Artichoke Croquettes

When my grandmother cooked these crocchette *for us as children we would crowd into the kitchen to eat them straight from the frying pan and never leave any for those at the table. There are many versions of these delicious little croquettes, but this one has the best flavour of all.*

4-6 globe artichokes
Salt
5ml/1 tsp extra virgin olive oil
Freshly ground black pepper
50g/2oz (⅓ cup) cooked ham, diced
2 egg yolks
1 egg, beaten
100g/3½oz (2¼ cups) fine breadcrumbs
Sunflower oil for deep-frying
For the béchamel sauce:
35g/1½oz (3 tbsp) butter
50g/2oz (3 tbsp) flour
300ml/½ pint (1¼ cups) milk
Salt and freshly ground black pepper
Freshly grated nutmeg
50g/2oz (½ cup) freshly grated Parmigiano
  Reggiano

Wash the artichokes and remove the outer leaves. Cut off the tips and the stalk at the base. Cut each artichoke lengthways into quarters, removing any trace of choke. Cook in a pan of boiling water with a pinch of salt and the olive oil until tender. This should take 25–30 minutes at the most.

Meanwhile, make the béchamel sauce. Melt the butter in a small saucepan over a very low heat. Remove from the heat and stir in the flour carefully. Add the milk little by little. When it has been incorporated and the mixture is smooth, return to the heat. Continue to stir well until the sauce thickens. Season with the salt, black pepper and nutmeg and stir in the Parmesan. When the artichokes are cooked, drain and work in a food processor until smooth. Season the artichoke purée with salt and black pepper, then remove from the processor and add the ham and the 2 egg yolks. Fold in the béchamel sauce and leave to cool.

When cold, mould into small round balls, dip in the beaten egg and then coat with breadcrumbs. Deep fry in very hot sunflower oil for about 2 minutes, until golden brown all over. Remove with a slotted spoon and drain on kitchen paper. Serve immediately. Serves 4

Melanzane Ripiene
Stuffed Aubergines

This is another recipe from our chef Tonino Punzi, who cooks with me in the summer in Apulia. I like to serve a dish of stuffed aubergines (eggplants), sweet peppers (capsicums) and courgettes (zucchini), each with a different filling. Of the three, aubergines are my favourite and taste even better cold the next day.

5 aubergines (eggplants)
Sunflower oil for deep frying
180ml/6fl oz (¾ cup) extra virgin olive oil
180ml/6fl oz (¾ cup) white wine
Salt and freshly ground black pepper
350g/12oz stale country bread, soaked in
  warm water
60ml/4 tbsp capers
50g/2oz (½ cup) freshly grated Parmigiano
  Reggiano – the best Parmesan cheese
2 eggs, beaten
A small bunch of fresh flat-leaf (continental)
  parsley, chopped
4 fresh tomatoes, skinned and chopped
2 garlic cloves, chopped
4 tbsp tomato sauce, see page 44, or chopped
  fresh tomatoes

Preheat the oven to 200°C/400°F/gas mark 6.

Cut the aubergines in half lengthways. Scoop out and reserve the pulp. Deep fry the skins in sunflower oil until golden; remove and drain on kitchen paper.

In another pan fry the chopped pulp in half the olive oil for about 5–8 minutes or until it softens, then add the wine and season with salt and black pepper. Cook for a further 5 minutes. Remove from the heat and cool.

In a large bowl mix the soaked and squeezed bread with the pulp, capers, most of the Parmesan, the eggs, parsley, chopped tomatoes and garlic. Check the seasoning. Fill the aubergine skins with this mixture. Oil a large roasting pan or oven dish, and cover the bottom with the tomato sauce. Put the aubergines in the dish, sprinkle Parmesan over the top and bake for 20 minutes. Serves 6

Other vegetables can be stuffed using this method, with the following variations: Courgettes (zucchini): Par-boil whole for 3–4 minutes, then trim the ends, cut in half lengthways and scoop out the insides. Replace the capers with a small bunch of chopped mint. Sweet peppers (capsicums): Cut the peppers in half, remove the seeds, and roast for 15 minutes. Stuff as in the recipe above, but replace the capers with 6 anchovies in olive oil, chopped small, and sauté 1 sweet pepper, finely chopped, to add to the mixture.

Pizza di Patate Pugliese

Potato Pizza from Apulia

Another sunny dish from Apulia, full of the favourite local ingredients. Like many other Apulian dishes, this is delicious hot or eaten cold the following day. You can serve this in wedges as a primo piatto *instead of pasta or rice.*

1kg/2lb potatoes
180ml/6fl oz (¾ cup) extra virgin olive oil
1 onion, cut in thick slices
8 ripe tomatoes, chopped
Salt and freshly ground black pepper
Fresh oregano
100g/3½oz (⅔ cup) black olives, pitted
3 canned anchovies, drained of oil and
*   chopped*
60ml/4 tbsp capers, rinsed and chopped

Preheat the oven to 200°C/400°F/gas mark 6.

Boil the potatoes, with their skins on, and when cooked, drain and peel. Mash to a rough purée with a potato masher or fork, adding about 60ml/4 tbsp of the olive oil.

In a frying pan heat about 30ml/2 tbsp of olive oil and lightly sauté the onion, adding the tomatoes after about a minute. Let this sauce simmer for about 10 minutes and then season with salt, black pepper and oregano.

Oil an oven dish or baking pan and line it with half the potato mixture. Spread a layer of the tomato sauce over this and sprinkle with the olives, anchovies and capers. Cover the tomato layer with the other half of the potato mixture. Drizzle with the remaining olive oil, and bake for 20 minutes until the top becomes golden. Serves 4–6

Sformato di Funghi
Mushrooms and Cream Mould

Italy is well known for its porcini mushrooms, which are used both fresh and dried. Every region has its own way of cooking them, and this recipe comes from Lombardy where I grew up, and where I spent many days picking funghi in the mountains. The richness of this dish is typical of this region, where butter, cream and all dairy products are used in profusion, and where olive oil only appears as a dressing for vegetables.

1kg/2lb mixed fresh mushrooms
10g/½oz dried porcini mushrooms, soaked
100g/3½oz (7 tbsp) butter
1 small onion, chopped
1 garlic clove, chopped
180ml/6fl oz (¾ cup) dry Marsala or
    medium dry sherry
200ml/6½fl oz double cream (¾ cup + 2 tbsp
    heavy cream)
1 egg yolk, beaten
Salt and freshly ground black pepper
50g/2oz (½ cup) Emmenthal cheese, grated
For the béchamel sauce:
50g/2oz (4 tbsp) butter
75g/3oz (4 tbsp) flour
450ml/¾ pint (2 cups) milk
Salt and freshly ground black pepper
Freshly grated nutmeg
50g/2oz (½ cup) freshly grated Parmigiano

Preheat the oven to 200°C/400°F/gas mark 6.

Make the béchamel sauce. Melt the butter in a small saucepan over a very low heat. Remove from the heat and stir in the flour carefully. Add the milk little by little. When the mixture is smooth, put the pan back on the heat. Continue to stir well until the sauce thickens. Season and stir in the Parmesan.

Clean the fresh mushrooms with a damp cloth and slice lengthways. Drain the porcini. In a saucepan, heat the butter and sauté all the mushrooms, the onion and garlic over a moderate heat. After a few minutes add the Marsala and cook slowly until the mixture has reduced. Add the cream and simmer until it reduces. Stir in the egg yolk and the béchamel sauce and season well. Butter a terracotta or other oven dish, pour in the mushroom mixture and sprinkle the Emmenthal evenly on top. Bake for about 20 minutes until the top has turned golden. Serves 6

Cipolle al Forno

Baked Onions

The simplest of vegetables are presented with maximum flavour in this easy recipe. Baking the onions whole, in their skins, seals in the juices and flavour.

4-6 white or red onions
Salt
Extra virgin olive oil
Freshly ground black pepper
25g/1oz (¼ cup) freshly grated Parmigiano Reggiano - the best Parmesan cheese

Preheat the oven to 200°C/400°F/gas mark 6.

Wrap each unpeeled onion in foil and place in a roasting pan with a layer of salt scattered over the bottom to absorb moisture. Bake in the oven for 30–45 minutes or until soft. Remove from the oven and unwrap the foil. When cool enough to handle, trim the ends of the onions and peel away the outer skins.

Lightly oil a baking tray with olive oil. Cut the onions horizontally in half and lay them on the tray, cut side up. Sprinkle with salt, black pepper and Parmesan, then drizzle a little olive oil on top. Return to the oven to bake for about 15 minutes until the tops begin to turn golden. Serves 4–6

Fave e Cicoria

Broad Beans and Chicory

One of the oldest Apulian dishes, this was intended to be a meal in itself. The broad beans are rich in protein and a good substitute for meat, which has always been scarce in the south. The green chicory provides a delicious contrast to the flavour and texture of the mashed beans, the whole enhanced by olive oil and lemon juice. Serve warm or cold as a primo piatto *instead of pasta or rice, but do not serve hot.*

For the broad bean purée:
450g/1lb dried broad beans (2½ cups dried fava beans), soaked overnight
180ml/6fl oz (¾ cup) extra virgin olive oil
Juice of 2 lemons
Salt
For the chicory purée:
700g/1½lb green parts of wild chicory leaves or spinach
180ml/6fl oz (¾ cup) extra virgin olive oil
Juice of 1 lemon
Salt

For the bean purée: Drain the beans and simmer in fresh water until they begin to break up and become thick and soupy in texture. This should take from 45 minutes to 1 hour. Drain, and work in a food processsor until they are smooth and velvety in texture. Transfer to a terracotta bowl (metal will make the purée discolour), stir in the olive oil and lemon juice with a wooden spoon, and season with salt.

For the wild chicory purée: Wash the chicory and wilt it in a large covered saucepan for 2 or 3 minutes – it should cook in the little water remaining on the leaves, but if there is any danger of burning, add a spoonful or two of water. When cooked, work in a food processsor until very smooth. Add a quarter of the bean purée. Stir thoroughly, and then work in the olive oil, lemon juice and salt. Transfer to a separate terracotta dish.

Drizzle the top of both purées with a little olive oil. Leave at room temperature for at least half an hour before serving. Serve generous spoonfuls of the two purées side by side. Serves 6

(see picture opposite)

Puree di Patate con Menta e Basilico

Potato Purée with Mint and Basil

Simple mashed potatoes are transformed into a very sunny Mediterranean dish with the addition of fresh herbs and olive oil. When I first made this last summer I was amazed at how good it was, and since then I have avoided ordinary mashed potato.

1kg/2lb potatoes
A generous handful each of mint, basil, flat-leaf (continental) parsley and sage, all chopped
270ml/9fl oz (1 cup + 2 tbsp) olive oil
Salt and freshly ground black pepper

Preheat the oven to 200°C/400°F/gas mark 6.

Boil the potatoes with the skins on and, when cooked, drain and peel. Mash or, ideally, push them through a potato ricer or sieve into a large bowl. Gently mix in all the herbs, the olive oil, salt and black pepper – try not to overwork the potatoes or they may lose their fluffiness. Oil a glass or terracotta ovenproof dish and transfer the potato mixture to it, spreading it out evenly. Drizzle with a little olive oil and bake for 15 minutes, until the potato mixture rises and the top turns golden. Serves 4–6

Dolci. Finishing a meal with some light and delectable pastry is heaven for me. These days Italians end their meals with fruit – peaches, pears, grapes, figs and pomegranates, arranged in simple abundance for the table. But on special occasions rich desserts make their appearance – for birthdays, family gatherings, local feste, saints' days and the main festivals of the Christian year. In farmhouses and country villas, Italian families celebrate with their own delicious concoctions of chestnuts and cream, chocolate and liqueur or intensely flavoured pastries. For centuries Italy has been famous for frozen confections, especially semifreddi and ice creams. Both cakes and ice creams are eaten to round off a meal, but also as little snacks in the middle of the morning, the afternoon, or late in the evening. A slice of cake and a glass of wine is a very homely Italian indulgence.

Pasta Frolla con Albicocche e Amaretti

Apricot and Amaretti Tart

I love desserts. This biscuity apricot tart is one of my favourites. You can substitute fresh peaches or pears for the apricots.

For the pastry:
280g/10oz plain flour (2 cups all-purpose flour)
A small pinch of salt
120g/4¼oz caster sugar (½ cup + 2 tbsp superfine sugar)
150g/5oz (10 tbsp) butter
1 whole egg
2 egg yolks
For the filling:
14 ripe apricots, or 6 peaches or 6 very ripe pears, peeled
24 amaretti biscuits (cookies), broken into small pieces
Grated zest of 1 lemon
Preheat the oven to 180°C/350°F/gas mark 4.

Make the pastry: sift the flour, salt and sugar into a large bowl. Rub in the butter. Add the egg and egg yolks and knead lightly to make a smooth dough. (This can also be made in a food processor). Wrap in plastic film and put to rest in the refrigerator for 30 minutes.

While the pastry is resting, prepare the filling: halve the apricots and put them in a bowl with the amaretti and lemon zest.

Roll out the pastry and use to line a 25cm/10 inch flan dish or tart pan. Add the filling, arranging the apricots rounded side up. Bake for 30–45 minutes. Serve warm or cold.
Serves 8

Torta di Cioccolato

Chocolate Cake

This couldn't be simpler or more delicious. The cake's soft inside is a revelation which will excite your senses. It works perfectly both on a rainy Sunday afternoon or during a warm summer evening. Chocolate cakes are very popular throughout Italy and people adjust the recipe to their own taste.

200g/7oz best-quality dark chocolate
100g/3½oz (7 tbsp) unsalted butter
4 large eggs
200g/7oz caster sugar (1 cup superfine sugar)
50g/2oz plain flour (2 tbsp all-purpose flour)

Preheat the oven to 140°C/275°F/gas mark 1.

Butter a round 25cm/10 inch cake pan and dust with flour. Melt the chocolate and butter in a bowl set over a pan of simmering water. Separate the eggs and put the whites to one side. Mix the egg yolks with the sugar and flour. Add the chocolate and butter and mix well. Beat the egg whites into soft peaks, and fold into the mixture very carefully to keep it light and airy.

Pour the cake mixture into the buttered pan and bake for 45 minutes. This flat soft cake is best served with a spoon. Serves 6

Tiramisù

Tiramisù

It took many experiments for me to find the exact proportions for this Tiramisù, which comes in the shape of a cake and is served in slices. Follow the quantities exactly and it will become a favourite.

600ml/1 pint (2½ cups) strong sweetened coffee
150ml/¼ pint (⅔ cup) dry Marsala or
medium dry sherry
4 egg yolks
75g/3oz caster sugar (3 tbsp superfine sugar)
2 x 500g/1lb 2oz tubs of mascarpone
2 packets spongefinger biscuits (ladyfingers)
or Italian savoiardi
Unsweetened cocoa powder

In a shallow dish mix the coffee with 30ml/2 tbsp of the Marsala. In a separate bowl, whisk the egg yolks and the sugar together until pale. Add the mascarpone to the egg mixture, one large spoonful at a time, mixing gently to keep the mixture light and airy. Add the remaining Marsala and mix in gently.

Dip about half of the biscuits into the coffee mixture and use to line the bottom of a 25cm/10 inch springclip cake pan. Spoon half the mascarpone mixture on top and sprinkle with cocoa powder. Repeat the layers. Chill in the refrigerator for at least 2 hours, then release the sping clip and serve sliced from the metal base. Serves 8

Pesche Ripiene
Stuffed Baked Peaches

Peaches are the very best of summer fruits in any Mediterranean country. They are delicious with just lemon juice or white wine, and they are equally good in a fruit tart (see page 114). In this recipe, which comes from my grandmother, they are very simply stuffed and baked. I usually serve them on their own, but they are also good with cold Greek or other thick yoghurt.

2 very ripe yellow peaches, peeled
14 amaretti biscuits (cookies), broken into pieces
50g/2oz caster sugar (2 tbsp superfine sugar)
A few drops of lemon juice
6 ripe yellow peaches, halved and stoned
A handful of peeled almonds, chopped

Preheat the oven to 180°C/350°F/gas mark 4.

In a bowl mash the peeled peaches with a fork until they are completely puréed. Add the broken amaretti, half of the sugar and the lemon juice. Work together until the mixture is amalgamated. Place the halved peaches, cut side up, in a buttered oven dish. Fill each of them with the amaretti mixture.

Sprinkle with the almonds and the remaining sugar. Bake for 30–45 minutes until they are golden on top but still retain their shape. Serve warm or cold. These will keep in the refrigerator, covered with plastic film, for 2 days. Serves 6

Crostata Fragolina con Mascarpone
Strawberry and Mascarpone Tart

*Strawberries are very good on top of this biscuity base, and combining them
with mascarpone makes for a smoother texture. The result is both delicious
and very pretty to look at.*

For the pastry case:
*280g/10¼oz plain flour (2 cups all-purpose
    flour)*
*120g/4¼oz caster sugar (½ cup + 2 tbsp
    superfine sugar)*
A pinch of salt
*160g/5½oz (11 tbsp) unsalted butter, in
    small pieces*
1 whole egg
1 egg yolk
For the filling:
1 egg yolk
50g/2oz icing sugar (3 tbsp confectioners' sugar)
30ml/2 tbsp dry Marsala or medium dry sherry
300g/11oz (about 1½ cups) mascarpone
250g/9oz strawberries

Preheat the oven to 180°C/350°F/gas mark 4.

Make the pastry: sift the flour, sugar and salt into a large bowl. Rub in the butter. Add the egg and the egg yolk and knead lightly to make a smooth dough. (This can also be made in a food processor.) Cover with plastic film and put to rest in the refrigerator for 30 minutes.

Roll out the pastry to fit a buttered and floured 25cm/10 inch springclip cake pan. Line the pan with the pastry and bake blind for 15–20 minutes. Leave to cool completely.

Beat the egg yolk with the icing sugar until pale. Add 30ml/2 tbsp of the Marsala, then add the mascarpone and stir with a wooden spoon until all the ingredients are amalgamated. Fill the cooled pastry case with the mascarpone mixture, spreading it out evenly. Arrange the strawberries on top and dust with more icing sugar before serving.
Serves 8

Budino Bianco
Cream Mould

Budini are moulded puddings, usually dark and made with chocolate. This lighter version is made with the delightful combination of rich cream and tangy Marsala.

3 sheets of gelatine, or 1 tbsp powdered gelatine
4 egg yolks
100g/3½oz caster sugar (½ cup superfine sugar)
120ml/4fl oz (½ cup) dry Marsala or
 medium dry sherry
30ml/2 tbsp brandy
250ml/8fl oz fresh double cream (1 cup
 heavy cream)

Soak sheet gelatine in cold water until very soft, then squeeze out excess water; soften powdered gelatine in 45ml/3 tbsp water until spongy. In a bowl, whisk the egg yolks with the sugar until pale. Then add the Marsala and the brandy, stirring in one spoonful at a time. Place the bowl in a pan half-filled with warm water over a gentle heat, so that the water just simmers. Keep stirring until the mixture begins to steam but does not reach boiling point. Remove from heat, add gelatine and stir in until it is completely melted. Leave to cool. When the mixture is cold and thick but not yet set, whip the cream and stir it in gradually to keep the mixture light. Pour the mixture into a shaped mould that has been sprinkled with some extra brandy. Cool and then leave to chill and thicken in the refrigerator for at least 3 hours or until set. Remove from mould carefully before serving. Serves 6

Crema Gelata al Limone

Chilled Lemon Cream

When I was 5 or 6 years old, I remember longing for this treat. I especially craved it after an illness or a visit to the dentist, when it made me feel better immediately. Nowadays I make it without even waiting to be ill and it has the same cheering effect.

3 eggs
75g/3oz caster sugar (3tbsp superfine sugar)
Grated zest of 3 lemons
360ml/12fl oz double cream (1½ cups heavy cream)
Lemon, icing (confectioners') sugar for dusting

Separate the eggs, and whisk the yolks with the sugar until pale. Beat the egg whites into stiff peaks, and mix very carefully with the lemon zest and yolk and sugar mixture. When all the ingredients are amalgamated whip the cream and fold in.

Pour the mixture into a freezer-proof bowl and freeze for at least 1 hour before serving. Decorate with lemon segments dusted in icing sugar. Serves 4–6

Zabaglione Freddo

Chilled Zabaglione

Zabaglione is every Italian child's dream. Somewhere in Italy there will always be a mother or grandmother beating egg yolks in the morning. This was a treat which I loved, and indeed still do. Here is a grown-up version, in which the addition of lemon zest reduces the sweetness and sharpens the tastebuds.

6 egg yolks
150g/5oz caster sugar (¾ cup superfine sugar)
180ml/6fl oz (¾ cup) dry Marsala
Grated zest of ½ lemon
300ml/½ pint double cream (1¼ cups heavy cream)

Put all the ingredients except the cream into a bowl set over a pan of simmering water. Beat vigorously while the mixture heats, until it becomes a thick creamy foam. Remove from the heat and allow to cool, stirring from time to time.

Whip the cream and fold into the cooled mixture very carefully. Serve in small glass dishes that have been chilled for 1 hour in the refrigerator. Serves 4–6

Gelato alle Pesche
Peach Ice Cream

Peaches, apricots and bananas are excellent for making ice cream. This one is as fresh, smooth and delicious as a peach itself. Serve it with crumbled amaretti on top.

400g/14oz ripe peaches, peeled and sliced
A few drops of lemon juice
1 whole egg
4 egg yolks
350g/12oz caster sugar (1¼ cups superfine sugar)
600ml/1 pint single cream (2½ cups light cream)
600ml/1 pint (2½ cups) milk

Purée the peaches in a food processor or with a fork, leaving them slightly chunky, and add a few drops of lemon juice. Stir the whole egg and the yolks in a large bowl with the sugar. Whisk until pale, and keep whisking while adding first the cream, then the milk.

Finally, add the peaches. If you are not using an ice cream machine, spoon into a shallow freezer-proof dish and freeze for about 1–2 hours until frozen but not solid. Every 15–20 minutes, stir the mixture gently until smooth and return to the freezer. Serves 6

Semifreddo ai Marroni
Chestnut Semifreddo

A semifreddo is a dessert with a high sugar and fat content which will not freeze hard. Chestnuts are used all over Italy, but the best ones come from Piedmont, near the Alps. This is a rich dessert that I can never bear to leave lingering in the refrigerator for too long.

2 egg yolks
50g/2oz caster sugar (2tbsp superfine sugar)
50g/2oz (2tbsp) unsweetened cocoa powder
500g/1lb 2oz marrons glacés, broken in pieces
600ml/1pint double cream (2½ cups heavy cream)

Whisk the egg yolks well with the sugar until pale. Add the cocoa powder and the crumbled *marrons glacés* and stir very gently.

Transfer to a serving bowl. Whip the cream and fold in a little at a time. Freeze for at least 2 hours before serving. Serves 6

Semifreddo al Miele con Uva e Noci

Semifreddo with Honey and Walnuts

This looks stunning and tastes heavenly. It fits exactly my idea of what a dessert should be.

600ml/1 pint double cream (2½ cups heavy cream)
180g/6oz (½ cup) honey - preferably
lavender or another flower honey
2 small pinches of cinnamon
50g/2oz (2 heaped tbsp) chestnut flower honey
30-45ml/2-3 tbsp warm water
400g/14oz mixed white and red grapes
6 walnuts, chopped

Put the cream, the bowl and the whisk in the freezer briefly: this will give you better results. Line the sides and the bottom of four individual round freezer-proof moulds with greaseproof (wax) or baking paper. Melt the lavender honey with 45ml/3 tbsp of the cream and the cinnamon over a gentle heat. Whip the rest of the cream and gently fold the melted honey mixture into it using a rubber spatula. Divide this mixture among the moulds and freeze for 6 hours until firm.

Before serving, melt the chestnut honey in the warm water. Wash and dry the grapes; remove seeds if necessary and cut the larger grapes in half. Mix with the walnut pieces.

Lift each semifreddo up out of the mould with the edges of the paper lining, and place in the middle of an individual serving dish. Remove the paper. Pour the grapes, walnuts and melted chestnut honey over the top of each and serve immediately. Serves 4

$\mathscr{I}$NDEX

ITALIAN COOKERY WEEKS has been running cookery courses in Umbria and Apulia for six years. The tuition and accommodation is located in lovely old buildings on farm estates where guests have the opportunity to learn the secrets of authentic Italian cookery while staying in stunning countryside, shopping in local markets and exploring historic towns. If you would like to know more, write directly to:

Italian Cookery Weeks, P.O.Box 2482, London NW10 1HW, Tel: 0181 208 0112 or Abercrombie & Kent, Holbein Place, London SW1, Tel: 0171 730 9600